Copyright Unbalanced

Copyright Unbalanced:
From Incentive to Excess

Edited by Jerry Brito

MERCATUS CENTER
George Mason University

ARLINGTON, VIRGINIA

ABOUT THE MERCATUS CENTER AT GEORGE MASON UNIVERSITY

The Mercatus Center at George Mason University is the world's premier university source for market-oriented ideas—bridging the gap between academic ideas and real-world problems.

A university-based research center, Mercatus advances knowledge about how markets work to improve people's lives by training graduate students, conducting research, and applying economics to offer solutions to society's most pressing problems.

Our mission is to generate knowledge and understanding of the institutions that affect the freedom to prosper and to find sustainable solutions that overcome the barriers preventing individuals from living free, prosperous, and peaceful lives.

Founded in 1980, the Mercatus Center is located on George Mason University's Arlington campus.

www.mercatus.org

Copyright © 2012 by Jerry Brito, Tom W. Bell, Eli Dourado, Timothy B. Lee, Christina Mulligan, David G. Post, Patrick Ruffini, and Reihan Salam

Mercatus Center
George Mason University
3351 N. Fairfax Drive
Arlington, VA 22201

Typeset by Sidecar Studio, Harrisonburg, Virginia. Composed in Max Miedinger's Helvetica Neue and Mitja Miklavcic's FF Tisa.

    Library of Congress Cataloging-in-Publication Data

Copyright unbalanced : from incentive to excess / edited by Jerry Brito.
    pages cm
  Includes bibliographical references and index.
  ISBN 978-0-9836077-5-5 (pbk.) -- ISBN 978-0-9836077-6-2 (ebook)
  1. Copyright--United States. I. Brito, Jerry.
  KF2994.C645 2012
  346.7304'82--dc23
                    2012045998

Second printing, with index, December 2012
Printed in the United States of America

Contents

1

Why Conservatives and Libertarians Should Be Skeptical of Congress's Copyright Regime

Jerry Brito

COPYRIGHT HAS LONG been a source of division among libertarians and conservatives. On one extreme are thinkers like Lysander Spooner, who believe authors and inventors should have perpetual property in their ideas. On the other are those like Tom Palmer, who reject intellectual property on the grounds that it conflicts with fundamental natural rights, including self-ownership. In between are those who accept some limited form of copyright, on both practical and moral grounds.

These are important philosophical distinctions. However, they often distract us from the political reality of our existing copyright regime. Whatever your philosophical position, if you are skeptical of government power, you should likewise be skeptical of the copyright system that has developed over the last century. That is, not necessarily skeptical of copyright in theory, but of the actual system that Congress has created and that it continues to expand.

You should be skeptical of Congress's ability to develop a rational policy given the knowledge problem copyright presents and the public choice pressures at work. You should be skeptical of the seemingly unlimited economic benefits we're told stronger copyright protection can produce, and you should instead be concerned about its effects on innovation. You should be skeptical of the recent trend toward criminal prosecution of even minor infringements of copyright law. You should be skeptical of the growing use of civil asset forfeiture in copyright enforcement. What follows in this book is not a moral case for or against copyright; it is a pragmatic look at the excesses of the present copyright regime and of proposals to further expand it.

Ayn Rand, a staunch proponent of copyright's morality, nevertheless noted that a "right to intellectual property cannot be exercised in perpetuity."[1] While she believed copyright is a moral imperative, she acknowledged that it must have limits or else "it would lead to the opposite of the very principle on which it is based: it would lead not to the earned reward of achievement, but to the unearned support of parasitism." Unfortunately, the exact contours of those limits cannot be divined through philosophical study, and are necessarily set down in law through a political process. And political processes, as any advocate of limited government knows, can be hijacked by the very "parasites" that so concerned Rand.

It is possible to have a deep respect for copyright—on moral or philosophical grounds, on the basis of economic efficiency, or for both reasons—and still recognize that a particular implementation of the idea of copyright can be flawed. Our current copyright regime should give conservatives and libertarians pause, if not make them shudder.

A DIFFERENT KIND OF PROPERTY

Whatever else you think about copyright, you must acknowledge that copyright is very different from traditional forms of property.

Traditional property rights, often associated with John Locke's theory of rights, include rights to real property, personal property, and property in one's self. The legitimacy of these rights is not just uncontroversial among libertarians and conservatives, it is foundational to their respective political ideologies.

Traditional property rights predate the Constitution, and their contours were developed over centuries in customary law and the iterative and evolutionary process that is the common law.[2] The main text of the Constitution doesn't even mention a right to property, signaling that the Framers took it for granted. Adding the Fifth Amendment, which says that one may not "be deprived of . . . property, without due process of law" and "nor shall private property be taken for public use without just compensation," the Framers again did not define property. That is because the Constitution was not *creating* a right to property; it already existed. The Constitution was merely recognizing it, and courts deciding cases under the Fifth Amendment would look to the common law for its definition.

Copyright is a very different animal. In contrast to traditional property, copyright was created by the Constitution; it did not exist in the common law. Without the Constitution's copyright clause, there would be no preexisting right in creative works. What's more, the copyright clause does not recognize an inalienable right to copyright, but instead merely grants to Congress the power to establish copyrights. Copyright therefore stands in contrast to traditional property in that the legislature has complete discretion whether to grant the right or not.[3]

The final and perhaps most peculiar difference between copyright and traditional notions of property can be found in their respective durations. The copyright clause allows Congress to establish copyrights for "limited times" only. This means that unlike traditional property, copyrights must cease to belong to their owners at a certain point. All this makes copyright a very different kind of property indeed.

WHAT'S THE DIFFERENCE?

Why is copyright so different from traditional property? One way to think about property in general is that it develops as a dispute-resolution mechanism. When a resource, such as land or game, is scarce or can be put to conflicting uses, disputes will result. Property rights emerge to settle these disputes.

For example, as economist Harold Demsetz pointed out in a seminal paper on property, Native Americans who hunted solely to feed and clothe their families had no need for property rights.[4] Game was sufficiently abundant so that it was not meaningfully scarce. However, once Europeans introduced the fur trade, the value of game increased and the scale of hunting rose sharply. The new relative scarcity of game gave rise to disputes about the allocation of game. Soon tribes developed property rights, which settled those disputes.

As Demsetz explained, property emerges as it becomes more worthwhile to internalize an externality. For example, before property rights, hunters could freely take as much game as they could kill. If they had done so, they would have overhunted and depleted the resource, making everyone worse off. Their individual actions would have imposed harm on others—a classic externality. Property rights address externalities by allowing an owner to take into account the harmful effects of an activity. That is to say, it is in an owner's interest not to overhunt, and indeed to invest in maximizing the sustainable stock of game.

Yet because they had no incentive to take as much as possible before the introduction of the fur trade, the Native American hunters could safely ignore the externality in their midst. Expending the resources necessary to establish and enforce property rights made no sense. Once the fur trade was introduced, however, the value of game increased and with it the incentive to overhunt—and the consequent disputes. Only then did it make sense for Native Americans to bear the costs of creating property rights, and that is indeed when they emerged. It became worthwhile to internalize the externality.

It is scarcity, or the possibility of conflicting uses, that leads to the spontaneous emergence of property rights. Informational goods, however, are not subject to such constraints.[5] If I write a song and you hear me sing it, you can later sing that song as much as you want without affecting my ability to sing it as well. Because the song can be sung by as many persons as want to sing it, without depleting anyone else's ability to do the same, there is no scarcity, and no possibility of conflicting use. As a result, property rights in information do not emerge spontaneously, and no common law develops.

WHY COPYRIGHT?

The fact that copyright does not emerge spontaneously does not mean it is illegitimate, or even unwise. What it does mean is that we should be cautious about how we create such a property right and how we define that right.

As F. A. Hayek showed, created orders are handicapped by the limited knowledge of their planners. This is in contrast to emergent orders, like customary or common law, which evolve slowly through trial and error. Such bottom-up processes are the product of human action, but not human design. As a result they incorporate dispersed knowledge and tend to match economic efficiency.

Copyright is a created order. Not only did it not emerge spontaneously, it is in fact a tool to *create* scarcity through state action. But why would we want to introduce scarcity where there is none? And why would we want to limit use where there is no conflict?

Like all other forms of property, copyright exists to address an externality problem. Because the author of a creative work, such as a song, cannot exclude others from the benefits her work creates, authors who publish works are creating a positive externality. The problem is that if authors can't internalize at least some of the positive externality they produce, then they will have only a weak incentive to create and publish works. Put another way, if authors have no way to exclude others from enjoying their works, and therefore can't charge users for access, then they won't produce as many works as they otherwise would, making everyone worse off. Copyright addresses this externality problem by creating a legal right to exclude others from enjoying the work without the author's permission. If authors can sell permission for money, they can capture a higher proportion of the benefits they create, and their incentive to produce creative works in the first place will increase.

By assigning authors property rights to their works, copyright allows authors to internalize some of the positive externality. Everyone is made better off. Certainly authors are, but so is the public, because it will enjoy an increase in the production of expressive works.

We can see in the copyright clause that addressing an externality is exactly what the Framers had in mind. The power the Constitution grants Congress is not the power to create copyright for the sake of copyright, or to give authors their just deserts, but specifically "to promote the Progress of Science and useful Arts." This is why the Supreme Court has said that "the copyright law, like the patent statutes, makes reward to the owner a secondary consideration."[6] Its main concern is ensuring that expressive works are available to the public.

A DELICATE BALANCING ACT

In many ways copyright is similar to emissions trading, also known as cap-and-trade. Like copyright, emissions trading addresses an externality problem, namely pollution. It does so by introducing scarcity where there was none before—the cap in cap-and-trade—and then leveraging markets to reach an efficient allocation of the newly limited "resource." Like copyrights, tradable emissions permits are a form of statutorily created property, which allow polluters to internalize the effects of their actions.

However, designing a new property right is a delicate balancing act. In the case of emissions, setting the cap too high may not reduce pollution by much. Setting the cap too low may reduce emissions by more than is necessary to address the environmental problem. What would be so bad about that? The answer is that there would be economic waste because you'd forgo more valuable emissions-producing activities, such as manufacturing, than necessary to protect the environment. (If the cap is set low enough, you might do away with manufacturing altogether.)

The same applies to copyright. If copyright is weak, then it will provide little incentive to create. But if it is too strong, then it will limit the public's ability to enjoy and build on creative works, which after all is the reason why we have copyright in the first place.

In either case there is a trade-off. Between clean air and cheap manufactured goods; between free access to creative expressions and providing an incentive to create. And not only is it possible to make the wrong trade, it's possible to make the wrong trade in either direction. That is, it's just as possible to trade away too much manufacturing for cleaner air as it is to trade away too much clean air for manufacturing. The trick is getting the right amount of each by striking the right balance. Get it wrong, and the result is waste and inefficiency.

COPYRIGHT'S KNOWLEDGE PROBLEM

The knowledge problem inherent in legislatively created rights is one reason why a delicate balance is difficult to reach. Not only are the contours of copyright centrally planned, but as Richard Epstein has noted, "There are in fact no 'natural' boundaries here, similar to the metes and bounds of land" to guide policy makers.[7]

Conservatives and libertarians tend to easily recognize the knowledge problems in other government programs. For example, consider subsidies for renewable energy, which are also arguably meant to promote the production of a public good.[8]

How does Congress know that the market is not already providing the right amount of investment in renewable energy? Without a government subsidy, there would still be investment in renewable energy technologies. By creating a subsidy, Congress is saying it doesn't think it's enough, but it has no way of truly knowing that.

Putting aside how Congress can know that there should be more investment in renewable energy, the other question is, how much investment is optimal? Without a market process to guide such investment, Congress can't know how much is enough. So when Congress offers a certain amount of subsidy, it's guessing.

It's likely offering too little or too much, with each error introducing its own inefficiencies.

The same challenges exist for copyright. Without copyright, there would still be songs written and movies made. Congress just thinks there wouldn't be *enough*. So, it offers a subsidy in the form of copyright protection to incentivize more creative output. The same questions we asked about renewable energy present themselves: How does Congress know we wouldn't have "enough" creative works without copyright? And assuming it knows that, how does it know the right amount of incentive to offer?

The first Copyright Act, which the Framers legislated, was limited to maps, charts, and books, which meant that other kinds of expressive works, such as songs and plays, were not protected. The Framers must have thought they would get enough such works without a subsidy. Were they wrong? Today songs and plays are protected, but fashion designs are not. Do we have the right balance now? How do we know?

The first Copyright Act also set a copyright term of 14 years renewable for 14 more, and required authors to register their works before receiving protection. Was 14 years enough, or too little? Today the copyright term is life of the author plus 70 years. Is that too much, or not enough? How do we know?

Also, requiring registration and renewal meant that only those authors who sought a subsidy got one. Only 5 percent of books published at the time were registered for copyright, and a small minority of their authors sought renewal, making the subsidy modest and somewhat self-regulating.[9] Today there is no requirement for registration or renewal, and anything you write is automatically protected whether you want it to be or not. Does such a massive trade of access for incentive get us closer to striking the delicate balance? How do we know?

This is not to say that because the ideal contours of copyright are unknowable, we should therefore have no copyright. After all, we also don't know that zero is the right amount of copyright. However, understanding that there is a knowledge problem in copyright is useful. It tells us that while Congress may inevitably have to make an educated guess when it designs copyright, it should be humble and not take lightly the possibility that it will strike the wrong balance and introduce serious inefficiency.

Unfortunately, humility and restraint are not qualities readily found in the modern Congress. As a result, we should question whether it has struck the right balance today. We should also question why Congress's quest for a delicate balance has required such massive trades in one particular direction.

COPYRIGHT'S POLITICAL PROBLEM

If the probability of striking the right balance for copyright didn't seem unlikely enough given the knowledge problem, consider then that the body charged with striking that balance is Congress.

The process by which the terms and scope of copyright are decided is a political one. This means that as it designs the contours of copyright, Congress will be picking winners and losers. Just as it might pick to subsidize solar- over nuclear-energy projects, Congress today has chosen to extend copyright protection to architecture and boat hull designs, for example, but not to fashion or aircraft designs.

It might be necessary for Congress to have such discretion in order to properly formulate a property right, but it also invites rent-seeking. Affected parties will undoubtedly invest resources to influence the design and enforcement of copyright with a goal of advantaging themselves and harming competitors—not benefitting the public, which is the object of copyright. Such activity is not only wasteful, it also makes it even less likely that Congress will do the right thing and strike the proper balance in its trade of access for incentive.

Retroactive term extension presents the clearest example of harmful rent-seeking in copyright. As we have seen, copyright's rationale is that potential authors are incentivized to create by having exclusive control of their works for some number of years.

You can imagine that Congress may want to lengthen this term if it finds that it has not created a sufficiently strong incentive to elicit "enough" creative productivity. But any such lengthening, one would think, should apply only to new works. After all, increasing the protection afforded to a work that has already been created can't possibly incentivize its author to create the work, for the simple reason that *it has already been created*. Yet this is what Congress has done time and again.

It seems like a joke, but each time the copyright on the Walt Disney character Mickey Mouse was about to expire, and the happy rodent was about to become a shared cultural icon like Santa Claus, Hamlet, and Uncle Sam, Congress has extended the copyright term not just prospectively for new works, but also retroactively for existing works. From the original 56 years it was entitled to under the 1909 Act, to life of the author plus 50 years in 1976, to life plus 70 years in 1998. If the pattern holds, we can expect another retroactive copyright term extension before the Mickey Mouse copyright expires in 2023.[10]

The problem is that Mickey Mouse already exists, and extending its copyright term cannot possibly incentivize Walt Disney to create Mickey Mouse. Not only is it a logical impossibility, but it's a sad fact that Walt Disney is dead, and increasing the protections afforded to his works can't possibly incentivize him to do anything.[11]

Retroactive term extensions do not serve the purpose copyright was originally intended to serve. They are nothing more than naked protections against competition, sought by the holders of existing copyrights. And not only can't retroactive extensions incentivize creators, but they also create a perverse incentive to invest in rent-seeking to acquire such extensions rather than investing in new creative work.

In Europe, the copyrights on the Beatles' first recordings were about to expire in 2013. Songs like "Love Me Do" would have joined classics like "Camptown Races" or "Danny Boy" in the public domain.[12] But music publishers lobbied for and got a 20-year retroactive term extension, stretching their government-granted monopoly on songs by the Beatles, Elvis, and many other popular musicians of the '60s until the 2030s. What the public got in return for this grant, if anything, is unclear.

And that's just it. Copyright's political problem is a classic case of concentrated benefits and diffused costs. Hollywood, the music industry, and book publishers reap the rewards of increased protection, while the public bears the costs. The copyright industries can easily organize themselves into lobbies that have every incentive to invest heavily in acquiring greater protections, while individual members of the public, the nominal beneficiaries of copyright, face a collective action problem that keeps them from organizing against stronger copyright laws.

Congress is supposed to represent the public's interest, but it has abdicated that responsibility. As Jessica Litman has carefully documented, Congress has turned over the responsibility of crafting copyright law to the representatives of copyright-affected industries.[13] That is, lobbyists write the copyright laws—not just figuratively, but literally.

For more than 100 years, copyright statutes have not been forged by members of Congress and their staff, but by industry, union, and library representatives who meet (often convened by the Copyright Office) to negotiate the language of new copyright legislation. As Litman explains, "When all the lobbyists have worked out their disagreements and arrived at language they can all live with . . . they give it to Congress and Congress passes the bill, often by unanimous consent."[14]

The public does not have a seat at the negotiating table, and Congress and the Copyright Office have tended to see copyright holders—not the public—as their constituents. What we have is capture, a government failure that conservatives and libertarians have long abhorred because it allows private parties to wield the power of government to grant privileges and limit competition. Copyright today is a public choice fiasco.

THE CONSEQUENCES

Copyright's knowledge and political problems result in a dysfunctional system that today looks more like an out-of-control government program, granting subsidies and privileges to special interests, than a rational system of statutory property. By almost any measure, copyright has exploded over the last 30 or 40 years, shifting the balance markedly in one direction.

"Terms of protection are longer, the number of things that are copyrightable has increased, it is easier to qualify for copyright protection, copyright owners have broader rights to control uses of their works, and penalties are harsher," writes Mark Lemley. "In addition, Congress has created entirely new rights."[15]

Perhaps worse is that in the name of further strengthening copyright, Congress has gone beyond establishing property rights and has moved to place restrictions on technology. The Digital Millennium Copyright Act of 1998 (DMCA), for example, criminalized the production or dissemination of technology that circumvents copy protection. The result is that while it was completely legal to make a backup copy of an analog VHS tape, it is now illegal to do the same with a DVD. As Christina Mulligan explains in chapter 5, the DMCA not only diminishes users' long-held rights to access information, but it also harms competition and free expression.

More recently, Congress attempted to pass the Stop Online Piracy Act (SOPA), which was defeated after vociferous online protests. That law would also have moved copyright policy into the realm of regulating technology. It would have required service providers to alter the Internet's Domain Name System to block allegedly infringing websites. As David Post explains in chapter 3, any benefits of increased copyright protection SOPA could have provided would have been outweighed by the damage it would have done to the Internet's technical and legal infrastructure.

Finally, the last decade or so has also seen a dramatic rise in the criminal enforcement of copyright, a departure from the traditional practice of civil suits by copyright holders against suspected infringers. Donald Harris has compared the current state of affairs to the

Prohibition era because law has outpaced societal norms.[16] There might also be a comparison to the drug war. As Tim Lee explains in chapter 4, the federal government now routinely employs civil asset forfeiture to seize the domain names, servers, and other assets of alleged infringers and online intermediaries. Such seizures take place before the owners are convicted of any crime and sometimes property is seized without the owners ever being charged.

Conservatives and libertarians, who are naturally suspicious of big government, should be skeptical of an ever-expanding copyright system. Congress today routinely shifts the copyright balance in only one direction: away from public access and freedom, and toward greater and deeper privileges for organized intellectual property interests. If we take economics and public choice seriously, then we should be concerned.

There is no incompatibility between respect for property and wariness of a radically unbalanced copyright system. Conservative politicians are beginning to understand this. As Reihan Salam and Patrick Ruffini point out in chapter 2, the anti-SOPA movement was led in part by Tea Party activists, and Republican members of Congress were the first to drop their support for the bill while Democrats like Al Franken defended it to the bitter end. After all, the entrenched interests copyright protects—Hollywood movie and music producers and New York publishers—tend to favor the political left.

Conservatives and libertarians should begin to think differently about copyright. We should ask ourselves, How much is enough protection? And how much is enough enforcement? As Eli Dourado points out in chapter 6, the system we have today likely far exceeds what we need in order to offer authors an incentive to create. And we should not only be skeptical of the inevitable calls for yet stronger protections, but we should seek serious reform as well. Tom Bell suggests in chapter 7 that perhaps the Framers got it right, and we should consider returning to the original Copyright Act.

If we can for a moment put aside our foundational disagreements about the nature of intellectual property rights, conservatives and libertarians may find that there is much agreement about the excesses and deficiencies of our current system. And we may also find that we are the best situated to lead a reform.

NOTES

1. Ayn Rand, "Patents and Copyright," in *Capitalism: The Unknown Ideal*, ed. Ayn Rand (New York: Signet Books, 1967), 131.

2. For a great discussion of the differences between customary and common law, see John Hasnas, "Hayek, Common Law, and Fluid Drive," New York University Journal of Law & Liberty 1 (2005): 79–110, http://www.law.nyu.edu/ecm_dlv3/groups/public/@nyu_law_website __journals__journal_of_law_and_liberty/documents/documents/ecm_pro_060886.pdf.

3. It should also be noted that it is unclear whether copyright is subject to the Fifth Amendment's takings clause. Thomas F. Cotter, "Do Federal Uses of Intellectual Property Implicate the Fifth Amendment?" *Florida Law Review* 50 (1998): 529, 532 (noting that the question "has evoked wildly differing responses, ranging from the view that virtually all government uses of intellectual property constitute takings to the view that virtually none of them do"). While the question remains undecided for copyright, the Federal Circuit in *Zoltek Corp. v. United States* recently held that the Fifth Amendment does not apply to patents. 442 F.3d 1345, 1350 (Fed. Cir. 2006). In that case, the court drew a distinction between traditional property and statutorily created patents, noting, "As the Supreme Court has clearly recognized when considering Fifth Amendment taking allegations, 'property interests . . . are not created by the Constitution. Rather, they are created and their dimensions are defined by existing rules or understandings that stem from an independent source such as state law.' Here, the patent rights are a creature of federal law." Ibid., 1352. This holding could suggest a similar outcome for copyright.

4. Harold Demsetz, "Toward a Theory of Property Rights," *American Economic Review* 57 (1967): 347–359.

5. As F. A. Hayek noted,

> The difference between [copyright and patents] and other kinds of property rights is this: while ownership of material goods guides the use of scarce means to their most important uses, in the case of immaterial goods such as literary productions and technological inventions the ability to produce them is also limited, yet once they have come into existence, they can be indefinitely multiplied and can be made scarce only by law in order to create an inducement to produce such ideas. Yet it is not obvious that such forced scarcity is the most effective way to stimulate the human creative process.

   F. A. Hayek, *The Fatal Conceit: The Errors of Socialism*, reprint edition (Chicago: University of Chicago Press, 1991), 36.

6. U.S. v. Paramount Pictures, 334 U.S. 131, 158 (1948).

7. Richard A. Epstein, "Why Libertarians Shouldn't Be (Too) Skeptical about Intellectual Property," Progress & Freedom Foundation Progress on Point Paper No. 13.4, February 2006, 8, http://papers.ssrn.com/sol3/papers.cfm?abstract_id=981779.

8. Of course, this is not a perfect analogy because subsidies for renewable energy tend to be granted to particular firms. Copyright, on the other hand, is made available to all.

9. Lawrence Lessig, *Free Culture* (New York: Penguin Press, 2004), 133.

10. It should be noted that Walt Disney got many of the characters and stories he used to make his films from the public domain, including Snow White, Sleeping Beauty, the three little pigs, and Robin Hood. This borrowing from the public domain to create new works is precisely the kind of cultural progress that copyright is meant to promote. In fact, the original copyright on Mickey Mouse comes from the character's first appearance in the film *Steamboat Willie* in 1928. That film, in turn, is a cartoon parody of the Buster Keaton film *Steamboat Bill Jr.* Walt Disney owed his success to his legitimate use of other's creations.

11. One could argue that the Walt Disney Company's ownership of the Mickey Mouse character continues to incentivize it to make new films

and products with that character. This is true, and if Disney were ever to lose its copyright on *Steamboat Willie*, that would not mean that Mickey Mouse would lose all protection. First, Disney would continue to receive copyright for any new original works starring Mickey. Second, Disney will always retain the trademark on Mickey Mouse, which allows it alone to make toys, lunch boxes, clothes, and other products featuring the mirthful mouse.

12. Bob Stanley, "Copyright Extension: Good for Cliff and the Beatles, Bad for the Little Guys?," *Guardian* (Manchester), September 15, 2011, http://www.guardian.co.uk/music/2011/sep/15/copyright-extension-cliffs-law-beatles.

13. Jessica Litman, *Digital Copyright* (New York: Prometheus Books, 2006).

14. Jessica Litman, "The Politics of Intellectual Property," *Cardozo Arts & Entertainment Law Journal* 27 (2009): 313, 314. The Sonny Bono Copyright Term Extension Act passed by unanimous consent. Ibid.

15. Mark A. Lemley, "Property, Intellectual Property, and Free Riding," *Texas Law Review* 83 (2005): 1031, 1042.

16. Donald P. Harris, "The New Prohibition: A Look at the Copyright Wars through the Lens of Alcohol Prohibition," *Tennessee Law Review* (forthcoming 2012), http://papers.ssrn.com/sol3/papers.cfm?abstract_id=2095193.

2

The Internet and Its Enemies

Reihan Salam and Patrick Ruffini

I N 2012, A number of institutions that have long defined American communication teeter near the brink of collapse. The US Postal Service struggles under the weight of crushing pension obligations as e-mail, Facebook, Twitter, and Skype render it all but obsolete. Across the country, major newspapers have stopped publishing. And strip-mall anchors from Circuit City to Blockbuster to Borders have filed for Chapter 11 bankruptcy protection.

In politics, traditional modes of wielding power are also being disrupted. One prominent example of this phenomenon is the recent battle over the Stop Online Piracy Act, or SOPA, in which grassroots activists defeated once-powerful Hollywood lobbyists.

What is toppling these formerly invincible companies and institutions? In almost every case, it is the Internet. Now we are engaged in a war over its future.

Unlike pro-Internet consumers, workers, and entrepreneurs, the Internet's enemies have been vocal, organized, and effective for a very long time. The fact that SOPA was defeated is the clearest indication that decentralized movements in favor of open markets and innovation can succeed despite this considerable disadvantage.

THE ULTIMATE ENTERPRISE ZONE

According to a McKinsey Global Institute study published last spring, 2 billion people worldwide are connected to the Internet, and almost $8 trillion changes hands via e-commerce every year.[1]

The United States captures 30 percent of all revenues generated by the global Internet economy, and 40 percent of the net income. Moreover, the Internet powerfully drives economic growth and job creation. In a survey of small and medium-sized enterprises, McKinsey found that for every job the Internet destroyed, 2.6 were created. In the advanced countries whose enterprises were surveyed, including the United States, Internet consumption and expenditure accounted for 21 percent of economic growth over the past few years.

One may be reminded of Jack Kemp's call in the 1970s and 1980s for "enterprise zones," in which eliminated regulations and lowered taxes spark entrepreneurship and growth in what were once blighted urban areas. The Internet is the ultimate enterprise zone. Just as Hong Kong's freedom and prosperity contrasted vividly with China's desperate poverty for much of the last century, the Internet stands out as an island of low regulation and taxation in a broader economy that grows less free with each passing year. The question is whether to allow Internet-enabled innovation to continue transforming the economy—dramatically reducing the cost and raising the quality of our education and health sectors, for example—or to allow the Internet's growth to be choked off by cronyism.

For now, the Internet represents the great exception to the rising tide of state-guided capitalism, in which the government favors politically connected firms and industries. As Ian Bremmer observes in his ominous book *The End of the Free Market*, the governments of the world's rising economies seek to dominate key economic sectors.[2] State-owned enterprises and sovereign wealth funds increasingly manipulate the global markets for energy, aviation, shipping, power generation, arms production, telecommunications, metals, minerals, petrochemicals, and much else.

Even the United States, long the bulwark of entrepreneurial capitalism, has moved in a dirigiste direction. During his recent State of the Union address,[3] President Obama celebrated the bailouts of GM and Chrysler, promising, "What's happening in Detroit can happen in other industries." What happened in Detroit? Taxpayers gave a massive cash infusion to politically connected corporations in a collapsing industry.

When we think of state capitalism, we tend to think of the Rust Belt, where automobile manufacturers and steel producers have clamored for bailouts and trade barriers for decades. But in the 21st century, handouts have gone to a wide range of industries, including the television and film production industries. Until 2001, only four US states had programs to encourage film production, typically through tax breaks and other giveaways. That year, the total amount offered was in the neighborhood of $1 million. Between 2001 and 2010, however, the number of states offering incentives climbed from four to forty, and the amount offered increased to $1.4 billion—note the change from m to b. Thankfully, a handful of states have abandoned their film-incentive programs since 2010, having recognized that they are a terrible deal for taxpayers.[4]

Yet film-incentive programs are just the tip of the iceberg. Hollywood has pursued numerous strategies to enrich itself at the broader public's expense, the most egregious of which includes the ongoing extension of copyright terms, as well as the criminalization of infringing copyright law and the expansion of federal resources devoted to its enforcement.

Article I, Section 8 of the US Constitution gives Congress the power "to promote the progress of science and useful arts, by securing for limited times to authors and inventors the exclusive right to their respective writings and discoveries." Congress has quietly acquiesced to several extensions of copyright terms over the past 35 years, with overwhelming, bipartisan support. Only with the 1998 Sonny Bono Copyright Term Extension Act did the unconstitutional nature of these extensions become too obvious to ignore. It is one thing to offer longer copyright terms to new works, "to promote the progress of science and useful arts," but extending the copyright terms of existing works simply allows incumbent firms to extract value from creators who expected their copyright to expire after a "limited" time. When asked to strike down the 1998 law, the Supreme Court declined; with uncharacteristic literal-mindedness, the Supreme Court noted that repeatedly extending copyright terms a few decades at a time does not make copyright unlimited. But one thing should be beyond dispute: endless copyright extensions violate the spirit of the Constitution.

Defenders of today's copyright regime, including at least some conservatives, insist that intellectual property be protected in the same way as any other kind of property. But as attorney and Bush-administration veteran Stewart Baker argues, copyright has come to resemble "a constantly expanding government program run for the benefit of a noisy, well-organized interest group."[5]

Before 1976, for example, one had to place a copyright notice on the title page of a book, file with the Copyright Office, and file to renew the copyright after 28 years, at which point the copyright term was extended for another 28 years. These requirements were hardly onerous, yet they helped manage the growth of copyright litigation by limiting copyright protection to those who explicitly sought it. Now, however, every work, including doodles sketched on a napkin, is automatically given copyright protection. This has led to an "orphan works" problem, in which works abandoned by their creators are left in legal limbo.

During the mid-1980s, Hollywood made a concerted effort to ban the VCR on the grounds that it was designed to facilitate copyright infringement. In the end, the courts decided that because the VCR had a substantial non-infringing purpose—to shift the time when people watched television programs—it should not be banned. But in 1992, the recording industry succeeded in pushing through the Audio Home Recording Act, which mandated that digital audio devices have industry-approved copyright protection built in. The new law also created a new tax on cassettes and other blank media designed to pay for the costs of piracy. In 1997, the No Electronic Theft Act dramatically increased the statutory charges for copyright infringement and, separately, the recording industry attempted to ban MP3 players, a bid that narrowly failed.

And in 1998, the Digital Millennium Copyright Act essentially gave the motion picture and recording industries veto power over the design of all digital media devices in the name of controlling piracy. The DMCA is why DVD players will not permit consumers to fast-forward through commercials at the start of a film. The Prioritizing Resources and Organization for Intellectual Property (PRO-IP) Act of 2008 represented yet another expansion of copyright protection. Taken together, this wave of legislation and litigation has helped destroy a number of innovative business models, including MP3.com, an early-2000s service that aimed to allow consumers to listen to their own legally purchased CDs while on the road.

And the Obama administration greatly expanded the federal government's efforts to protect copyright holder interests, tasking the overburdened Bureau of Immigration and Customs Enforcement with seizing foreign websites accused of copyright infringement.[6]

RENT-SEEKING AND INNOVATION

Just as copyright terms are growing longer and more restrictive, patent rights are strengthening. As George Mason University economist Alex Tabarrok argues, unyielding patents reduce innovation. In *Launching the Innovation Renaissance*, Tabarrok observes how strong intellectual-property protections can create a "resting on laurels" effect.[7] Rather than investing in innovation to outcompete rivals, firms stockpile patents and attack potential competitors with lawsuits. The technology industry now diverts billions from research and development to acquire patent portfolios. As Microsoft founder Bill Gates presciently warned in 1991, "I feel certain that some large company will patent some obvious thing" and use the patent to "take as much of our profits as they want."[8] Microsoft, alas, now plays the role of the large company, as do innumerable patent trolls.

This situation, in which rent-seeking behavior trumps innovation, is where Hollywood finds itself today. As consumers and entrepreneurs seek new, more convenient ways to consume media, Hollywood fights desperate rearguard actions, forcing people to consume media in ways that serve Hollywood, not themselves.

The industry's prodigious success translating glitz, glamor, and timely campaign contributions into political influence lulls it into the belief that the federal government can keep it afloat despite a lack of innovation. While Hollywood failed to ban the VCR and the MP3 player, it succeeded in suing out of existence MP3.com and the streaming-film services Kaleidescape and Zediva. These suits are especially troubling since they represent a largely successful attempt to keep the "first sale" doctrine of copyright law—the basis for everything from libraries to Netflix mail order—from applying to streaming media.

The entertainment industry claims, correctly, that media piracy has increased over the last decade. Last summer, a survey sponsored by the American Assembly, a public-affairs forum affiliated with Columbia University, found that 46 percent of US adults had acquired unauthorized music or video, and that percentage rose to 70 among those younger than 30.[9] But only 2 percent had acquired *most* of their media collections through piracy, and the emergence of legal streaming-music and streaming-video services has curbed the appetite for unauthorized content. The emergence of Netflix's streaming-video service, for example, coincided with a marked decline in the number of searches for BitTorrent, a favorite protocol for exchanging pirated media. The convenience of iTunes has similarly reduced piracy as a share of digital-media consumption. Last year, the Social Science Research Council published "Media Piracy in Emerging Economies," the most comprehensive study of the piracy problem to date.[10] The report, notably not funded by the entertainment industry, concludes that business-model innovation, not heavy-handed legislation, curbs media piracy.

Big Media's reluctance to embrace business-model innovation is understandable: the old model was incredibly lucrative. Between 2000 and 2010, the domestic revenues of the recorded music industry were cut in half.[11] Some of this decline was the direct effect of piracy, but by far most of it was the business-model innovation of iTunes and similar digital downloads markets. The secret weapon of the CD (and before that, LP) business had always been that you couldn't buy the single you heard on the radio without buying another ten to fourteen tracks that didn't really interest you. iTunes changed all that by allowing customers to buy singles for $1 or so and not surprisingly the customers usually pass on buying the rest of the album.[12] This is a long-standing pattern in copyright industries: pirates introduce a new business model at a low price point (e.g., Napster and MP3s) and the industry at first attempts to suppress the pirates (e.g., getting injunctions against Napster) but eventually resigns itself to adapting to the new business model (e.g., iTunes).[13]

However, while recorded music revenues may be down, by many other metrics popular entertainment shows great vitality. Michael Masnick, a blogger and venture capitalist with a leading role in technology-policy debates, released "The Sky Is Rising," a 2012 report on how the rise of digital consumption changed the entertainment industry.[14] Between 2005 and 2010, the global music industry increased in value from $132 billion to $168 billion. Despite a weak economy, the share of total household spending devoted to entertainment increased by 15 percent in the US over the same period. US entertainment industry employment increased by 20 percent from the late 1990s to the late 2000s, in part because of an explosion of activity that occurred outside the largest media companies. In short, the industry is booming.

The entertainment industry relies heavily on the notion that piracy devastates artists. Yet it turns out that piracy primarily hurts legacy media firms reluctant to embrace the digital revolution; artists willing to adapt to the new environment, and to the consumer desire for more direct relationships with artists they admire, have flourished. According to the Bureau of Labor Statistics, the number of independent artists increased by 43 percent from 1998 to 2008 as it grew easier to generate income without signing with a major recording company.[15] This independence might prove particularly advantageous to artists who appeal to culturally conservative consumers, a market niche that the big media companies tend to neglect.

Essentially, Big Media are trying to enlist the federal government in an effort to save their failing business model under the pretense of protecting artists and workers. Like the Big Three automakers, these companies want a bailout. Until recently, they had reason to think they'd get one. After all, while the entertainment industry failed to persuade the federal government to ban the VCR in the 1980s, and the MP3 player in the 1990s, it has managed to deploy government power against a number of similarly promising web-based technologies. To be sure, many of these technologies can indeed facilitate copyright infringement, and more aggressive enforcement might reduce infringement. But it is far from obvious that taxpayers have an unlimited interest in reducing infringement, particularly as the strategies for doing so grow ever more expensive and intrusive.

Yet Hollywood contributes vast sums to political candidates, particularly on the left, through the influential lobbies of the Motion Picture Association of America and the Recording Industry Association of America. For decades they won almost every political battle they joined, in part because they tended to strike deals behind closed doors. The winning streak, however, has come to an end.

GOP OPPOSITION TO SOPA: FROM PRO-BUSINESS TO PRO-MARKET

At the outset of the most recent legislative debate over online piracy, Hollywood was poised to extend its flawless copyright-expansion win streak. Under the guise of blocking foreign "rogue" websites, the Protect IP Act, or PIPA, an earlier Senate counterpart to SOPA, achieved levels of bipartisan cosponsorship unseen in all but 19 other Senate bills (out of 1,900), according to OpenCongress .org. In May 2011, the legislation passed the Judiciary Committee by voice vote, without hearings. There was no reason to think that the House version, which became SOPA, would be any different.

But when House Judiciary Committee chairman Lamar Smith (R-TX) delivered the bill in late October, alarm bells went off in startups and venture-capital firms throughout Silicon Valley and New York City. Brad Burnham, a cofounder of Union Square Ventures and the first institutional investor in Twitter, helped mobilize the early protests, which would inspire the larger blackouts of Wikipedia, Reddit, and more than 100,000 other websites in January of 2012. "The infrastructure of the Internet, chips, routers, and microprocessors were conceived and created a long way from Washington, and the entrepreneurs and investors who built those businesses liked it that way," Burnham reflected. "Politics had little impact on this insulated world." But slumber was no longer an option: An industry that had shunned lobbyists now paid the price. The legislation placed a business model that allows users to freely share content without prescreening or approval (the basis of the modern Internet) in legal jeopardy. (The original version of SOPA aimed to criminalize sites taking "deliberate actions to avoid confirming a high probability" of copyright violations.)

December's House markup hearings fully displayed Congress's blithe aspiration to regulate an industry it did not understand. SOPA proponents professed ignorance of the Domain Name System, a fundamental piece of Internet architecture they proposed to radically alter. North Carolina Democrat Mel Watt, one of the bill's early sponsors, memorably confessed, "I'm not a nerd."[16]

To the tech community, stopping SOPA became a life-or-death struggle. On top of its DNS censorship provisions, SOPA sought to require search engines to censor results pointing to sites merely accused of piracy and grant legal immunity to Internet Service Providers that would voluntarily block access to accused websites.

Ultimately, the indictment of SOPA as a complex regulatory boondoggle may prove more instrumental to its collapse than the Internet's cries of censorship. So suggests Republican lawmakers' decision to dump the bill en masse.

Like most examples of Beltway cronyism, SOPA was the product of an out-of-touch bipartisan lobbyist elite, who understood precious little about the networked and decentralized medium they proposed to regulate. This elite badly underestimated the political power of an "Internet public" connected by social media and smartphones. A guerrilla force of techies and populists, ranging across the political spectrum from MoveOn.org to the Tea Party Patriots, joined forces to mount an unconventional assault on Hollywood's lobbying arm, which had spent $94 million lobbying for copyright legislation in 2011. The result: the January 18 web blackout that prompted millions of calls to Capitol Hill, forced dozens of lawmakers to switch sides, and consigned SOPA to the dustbin of history—for now.

After both sides of the SOPA debate were heard, conservatives were quicker to rally to the side of the rebels. At one point, hours into the Internet blackout, 26 of the 29 legislators who switched sides were Republicans. Minnesota Democrat Al Franken, who had fashioned himself the Senate's chief defender of the "open Internet," e-mailed supporters defending the Protect IP Act in the name of "middle class workers—most of them union workers," who work in copyright-dependent industries.[17] Franken, himself a card-carrying member of the Screen Actors Guild, represented in microcosm the coalition of Hollywood and labor threatened by the disruptive forces of technology. Senator Chuck Schumer and Representative Kristen Gillibrand, both New York Democrats, privately seethed at Republicans who withdrew their cosponsorship, among them Florida Republican senator Marco Rubio.[18]

Behind the scenes, Republicans used the piracy debate to register their displeasure at Harry Reid's imperious management of the Senate. When Reid put the Protect IP Act on the Senate floor schedule, the bill's main Republican proponents were not even consulted. A few days before the scheduled floor vote, a group of Republican senators, including chief Republican sponsor Chuck Grassley and Utah conservative Mike Lee, called on Reid to delay consideration of the bill indefinitely.[19]

Republican opposition to SOPA, though influenced by many factors, is rooted in conservative skepticism about the imposition of regulations rigged to favor powerful corporate insiders. This skepticism wasn't on display for most of the Bush era, when many in the GOP reconciled themselves to being part of a pro-business rather than a pro-market and pro-freedom political movement. Public hostility to the Wall Street bailouts, and the rise of the Tea Party, provided a useful corrective—and conservatives in Congress now wish to be on the side of consumers and the entrepreneurs who serve them, rather than that of crony capitalists who use state power to extract rents.

A RADICAL ALTERNATIVE TO CRONY CAPITALISM

Stifling Internet innovation is not restricted to media companies; rather almost every established industry that fears disruptive change has sought to build barriers to block Internet-enabled competition. Real estate agents, mass-transit agencies, cab companies, and purveyors of wines and spirits are just a few of the special interests that have tried to regulate away competition by web entrepreneurs.

Perhaps the most important example of an Internet-phobic industry is the education sector. All over the country, teachers' unions fight bitterly against online-education efforts that promise to lower the cost and improve the quality of instruction. Traditional colleges and universities wage rearguard actions against online universities that offer "all you can eat" pricing plans, which allow students to take as many courses as they can handle for a flat fee. The medical profession, similarly, is reluctant to embrace Internet-enabled technologies that empower patients and in the process drive down costs. Sectors such as health care and education, in which political imperatives trump market competition, are most plagued by inefficiency. Fortunes are made not by meeting consumer needs, but by securing political favors.

The Internet represents a radical alternative to crony capitalism. Larry Downes, a right-leaning technology analyst and one of the most insightful chroniclers of the fight against SOPA, described what he calls "the political philosophy of the Internet": "Its central belief is the power of innovation to make things better, and its major tenet is a ruthless economic principle that treats information as currency, and sees any obstacle to its free flow as inefficient friction to be engineered out of existence."[20] The belief he describes is rooted in the Internet's open, meritocratic nature. And it is a belief very much in keeping with core conservative values.

The Internet, and the phenomenal success of technology entrepreneurs like Steve Jobs, Mark Zuckerberg, Sergey Brin, Larry Page, and countless others, are vivid examples of markets at their best. The world's most deregulated industry has, not coincidentally, seen corporate empires rise and fall with astonishing speed. Yet the chief beneficiaries aren't Silicon Valley billionaires. Rather, they are citizens, workers, and consumers with the power to choose new ways of living, working, and consuming.

We have described the Internet as our Hong Kong, our beacon of economic freedom. But whereas the Mainland swallowed up Hong Kong, there is a chance that the dynamism of the Internet could take over and revitalize our overtaxed, overregulated, moribund economy.

Achieving this larger goal will require a more ambitious set of reforms. The anti-SOPA coalition, for all its virtues, was ultimately a negative coalition that aimed to prevent a change its members perceived as destructive. What we need now is a reform movement devoted to taking on other barriers to innovation, like the glut of software patents and the expansion of copyright protectionism. In an era of sluggish economic growth, this could be a potent way for conservatives and libertarians to connect the cause of economic freedom to the promise of a more prosperous future.

NOTES

1. Jacques Bughin et al., *Internet Matters: The Net's Sweeping Impact on Growth, Jobs, and Prosperity*, May 2011, http://www.mckinsey.com /insights/mgi/research/technology_and_innovation/internet _matters.

2. Ian Bremmer, *The End of the Free Market: Who Wins the War between States and Corporations?* (New York: Penguin Group, 2010).

3. Barack Obama, "State of the Union 2012: Obama Speech Transcript," *Washington Post*, January 24, 2012, http://www.washingtonpost.com/politics/state-of-the-union-2012-obama-speech-excerpts/2012/01/24/gIQA9D3QOQ_story.html.

4. Joseph Henchman, "More States Abandon Film Tax Incentives as Programs' Ineffectiveness Becomes More Apparent," Tax Foundation, June 2, 2011, http://taxfoundation.org/article/more-states-abandon-film-tax-incentives-programs-ineffectiveness-becomes-more-apparent.

5. Stewart Baker, "Exclusionary Rules," *Wall Street Journal*, March 26, 2004, http://online.wsj.com/article/SB108019177856065188.html.

6. Josh Smith, "White House Reports Increase in Copyright Enforcement," *National Journal*, March 30, 2012, http://techdailydose.nationaljournal.com/2012/03/white-house-reports-increase-i.php; "2011 U.S. Intellectual Property Enforcement Coordinator Annual Report on Intellectual Property Enforcement," March 2012, http://www.whitehouse.gov/sites/default/files/omb/IPEC/ipec_annual_2011_report.pdf.

7. Alex Tabarrok, *Launching the Innovation Renaissance* (TED Books, 2011).

8. Bill Gates, Microsoft internal confidential memo, May 16, 1991, http://www.std.com/obi/Bill.Gates/Challenges.and.Strategy.

9. Joe Karaganis, "Copyright Infringement and Enforcement in the US," American Assembly (Columbia University), November 2011, http://piracy.americanassembly.org/wp-content/uploads/2011/11/AA-Research-Note-Infringement-and-Enforcement-November-2011.pdf.

10. Joe Karaganis, ed., "Media Piracy in Emerging Economies," Social Science Research Council, 2011, http://piracy.americanassembly.org/wp-content/uploads/2011/06/MPEE-PDF-1.0.4.pdf.

11. US Census Bureau, *Statistical Abstract of the United States*, 2012 (Washington, DC, 2011), 716.

12. Anita Elberse, "Bye-Bye Bundles: The Unbundling of Music in Digital Channels," *Journal of Marketing* 74 (2011): 107–23.

13. Barry Kernfeld, *Pop Song Piracy: Disobedient Music Distribution since 1929* (Chicago: University of Chicago Press, 2011).

14. Michael Masnick and Michael Ho, "The Sky Is Rising: A Detailed Look at the State of the Entertainment Industry," Corporate and Communications Industry Associates, January 2012.

15. Ibid.

16. Evan Niu, "Don't Mess with the Internet," *DailyFinance*, January 12, 2012, http://www.dailyfinance.com/2012/01/22/dont-mess-with -the-internet/.

17. Sen. Al Franken, in the series "SOPA Opera: Where Do Your Members of Congress Stand on SOPA and PIPA?," *ProPublica*, January 20, 2012, http://projects.propublica.org/sopa/F000457/.

18. Erica Orden and Geoffrey A. Fowler, "Hollywood Loses SOPA Story," *Wall Street Journal*, January 19, 2012, http://online.wsj.com/article /SB10001424052970204555904577168843130020190.html.

19. Press Office of Senator Mike Lee, "Lee Reaffirms Opposition to PRO-TECT IP Act," press release, January 18, 2012, http://www.lee.senate .gov/public/index.cfm/press-releases?ID=ba6375b8-e350-49da-aa62 -ce84d4e95939.

20. Larry Downes, "Who Really Stopped SOPA, and Why?," *Forbes*, January 25, 2012, http://www.forbes.com/sites/larrydownes/2012/01/25 /who-really-stopped-sopa-and-why/2/.

3

SOPA and the Future of the Internet

David G. Post

S O WHAT WAS all that fuss about? SOPA, PIPA, Internet Blackout Day, front-page stories in newspapers all across the country, 8 million or so emails pouring into the White House, 2 million #sopa tweets, and 10 million signatures added to online petitions opposing the bills—followed, of course, by the announcement that these various legislative proposals for combating online copyright and trademark infringement had all been taken off the table "for further study."

As Larry Downes noted in *Forbes*, "Internet users have revolted before in the face of earlier efforts to regulate their activities, but never on this scale or with this kind of momentum."[1]

What happened? How did it happen? And does it matter?

I'm not sure anyone can yet say exactly what happened or how it happened. But whatever it was—a spontaneous, grassroots outpouring of opposition to an attack on Internet freedom of expression, a bunch of information junkies who've gotten hooked on free music and free movies sticking it to The Man, or a plot by the giant technology companies to show Washington who's boss—I'm here to tell you that it matters, and it matters a great deal.

It matters because the Internet matters. If the events of the Arab Spring didn't finally persuade everyone of *that*, I can't imagine what would or will. SOPA would have done serious damage to the technical infrastructure that allows the Internet to do the remarkable things that it does.

And it matters because the law matters. We are currently in the early years—the very beginning, really—of our efforts to construct a just, meaningful, and effective legal order for the global network. History tells us that many of the decisions we make today about how that legal order is to be constructed will have deep and possibly irreversible consequences for us down the road—especially when those decisions raise truly fundamental questions about what law is and how it is to operate. SOPA raised just such questions.

And, finally, it matters because the law enforcement regime that SOPA would have put into place reflects an underlying vision and an approach to the problems of "Internet law" and "Internet governance" that is outmoded, unworkable, and unjust.

Understanding what that underlying vision is, and how it was implemented in SOPA, is thus of some considerable importance, allowing us to recognize it (and, one hopes, to fight it off once more) when and if it rears its ugly head again.

SOPA'S OBJECTIVE

SOPA's objective was straightforward: to eliminate (or at least re-duce) access to "foreign infringing Internet sites"—for example, offshore websites offering copyrighted music or movies for download, or selling counterfeit Rolex watches, without authorization from the rightsholders.[2]

There are many such sites, a fact that we can attribute to two very fundamental characteristics of the global network.

First and most obviously, digital information can be reproduced at nearly zero cost, and with nearly 100 percent accuracy, making it a simple matter to do something that was for all intents and pur-poses impossible a mere 20 or 30 years ago: say, produce 100,000 copies of the motion picture *Avatar* while on coffee break, and with a lower outlay of funds than is required for your cappuccino.

Second, physical proximity in realspace no longer bears any significant relationship to *accessibility* or to "proximity" on the network. In realspace—the world of atoms and tangible matter—it's harder to do business in London if you're in Lima than it is if you're in Liverpool, and it's harder to cause harm in Seattle from Seoul than from Spokane. But in the world of bits, that's just not true anymore; web servers in all those cities are effectively "equidistant" from one another, as "close to," and as accessible to, a user *anywhere* on the global network as the server down the street.

That's the good news! It's an astonishing engineering achievement—perhaps *the* astonishing engineering achievement—that helps to explain the Internet's extraordinary power and scope: (pretty much) everything that is available in digital form (pretty much) anywhere is now accessible to (pretty much) everyone (pretty much) everywhere.

The bad news, though, is that our existing legal infrastructure is, just as one would expect it to be, built for the world of atoms. (How could it have been otherwise?) Our legal system reflects the world within which it was designed to operate; precisely because physical location and physical proximity matter so much in realspace, they are indispensable components of many doctrines central to the operation of realspace law: "jurisdiction," "citizenship," the "locus" of a contract or a tort, and dozens of other similar notions. The physical distance between actors matters in our existing legal world because it matters in our realspace world; the more physically distant the relevant actors the more difficult it is, generally speaking, to enforce one's law on them.

To put it bluntly but not inaccurately: law (by and large) respects borders; the Internet (by and large) does not.

Mix together the infinite and inexpensive reproducibility of valuable digital goods, the irrelevance of physical location and physical proximity, and border-respecting law, and the results are fairly predictable; many people saw this coming.

That it was predictable does not, however, mean that it is not a profoundly difficult challenge: How do we bring law to this border-disrespecting place? Should we be striving to reconstruct those legally significant physical boundaries on the net? And if so, how do we do *that*? Should we be striving to develop a legal regime that abandons physicality altogether—and if so, how do we do that?

We will, somehow, have to solve this problem—at least, if we want the net to be a lawful place, as I take it we all do (and should). It will take considerable creative and innovative thinking to solve it in a just and sensible way.

SOPA reflects some creative and innovative thinking; indeed, it embodies a radical new plan for the way that law enforcement will proceed on the Net. But that plan is anything but just and sensible; it is deeply flawed, and would set us on precisely the wrong course for dealing with this most difficult challenge. While SOPA was defeated, the ideas it embodied have not gone away and will likely resurface in future legislative proposals.

HOW SOPA WOULD HAVE WORKED

SOPA would have targeted the activities of "foreign infringing websites,"[3] but not by imposing any sanctions on the offending websites, on the servers on which those websites are hosted, or even on the operators of those websites. Instead, SOPA would have imposed its sanctions on the *domain names* used by those websites.

More specifically, SOPA would have authorized federal prosecutors, and private rightsholders in certain circumstances, to bring *in rem* actions against the domain names associated with these sites—allowing the court, in effect, to "seize" the domain names for purposes of adjudicating the claims related to them. These *in rem* actions would be permitted whenever the owner or operator of the allegedly infringing website either (a) cannot be located (after "due diligence" on the complainant's part) or (b) is found but has no address "within a judicial district of the United States."[4] Having asserted jurisdiction over the *res*—the domain name—the court could proceed to a hearing at which it would evaluate the claim that the site in question is a "foreign infringing site," or one "dedicated to the theft of US property."[5] The court, on completing its evaluation of the evidence, could then issue an order to any US-based Internet Service Provider—a category that includes hundreds of thousands of entities, from giants like Comcast, Verizon, and AT&T

to any business or educational institution that offers Internet access to users—to remove the offending domain names from the its "routing tables," the databases of Internet domain names and Internet addresses used by all ISPs to get messages from one place to another over the net.[6]

WHAT SOPA WOULD DO TO THE INTERNET

Every day, the Internet accomplishes an astonishing feat, many hundreds of billions of times over: It takes an address on a message (like the URL that you type into your web browser, or the e-mail address you put into the appropriate field of an e-mail message), and, from among the 700 or 800 million machines out there on the Internet, it finds the right one to deliver it to. And it does all this, generally speaking, in no more than a second or two.

It is a truly incredible (and largely invisible and unappreciated) feat of engineering, a finely tuned system (to put it mildly) comprising, among other things, hundreds of thousands of copies of these routing table databases circulating around the Internet from ISP to ISP at all times.[7]

All that complicated engineering rests on a fundamental principle: *universal addressing*. The Internet routing tables should be the same wherever you are, and by and large they are. That's why, in a world in which there are thousands upon thousands upon hundreds of thousands of networks and inter-networks, there's only one "Internet," the single network that looks the same whether you access it from Birmingham or from Boston or from Brazzaville.

The principle, to be sure, is not sacrosanct, and is not always obeyed; the Internet most assuredly does not look the same in Beijing, or Belarus, as it does elsewhere. But while we have no choice but to tolerate these deviations, we need not, and we should not, emulate them. Court interventions ordering the selective removal of entries from these routing databases would have done just that with potentially severe and possibly catastrophic effects.

Don't take my word for it: a number of people who know a great deal more about these engineering matters than I do, several of whom were instrumental in creating the original design for the Internet's domain name system and who continue to manage and operate critical portions of the infrastructure, have warned about this in no uncertain terms. In their words, SOPA's court-ordered manipulation of the domain name system would

1. be "evaded easily" and "likely prove ineffective at reducing online infringement";
2. "threaten the security and stability" of the Internet, "harming efforts that rely on [Domain Name System] data to detect and mitigate security threats and improve network performance" and "posing significant risk of collateral damage"; and
3. "weaken important efforts now underway to improve Internet security [by] enshrining and institutionalizing the very network manipulation that [such security measures] must fight in order to prevent cyberattacks and other malevolent behavior on the global Internet, thereby exposing networks and users to increased security and privacy risks."[8]

As Internet Blackout Day approached, the Obama administration finally got the message. On January 14, in the face of mounting public pressure, the White House announced that it was reconsidering its support for SOPA, in part because

proposed laws must not tamper with the technical architecture of the Internet through manipulation of the Domain Name System (DNS), a foundation of Internet security. Our analysis of the DNS filtering provisions in some proposed legislation suggests that they pose a real risk to cybersecurity and yet leave contraband goods and services accessible online. We must avoid legislation that drives users to dangerous, unreliable DNS servers and puts next-generation security policies, such as the deployment of DNSSEC, at risk.[9]

Reassuring words—though one might ask why they hadn't been uttered earlier in the SOPA debate.

But the damage SOPA would have imposed on the Internet goes beyond this (though this is serious enough), extending beyond the Internet's technical infrastructure and deep into its legal infrastructure.

SOPA UNDERMINES THE RULE OF LAW

Two of SOPA's provisions are especially troubling. First, SOPA would have authorized the issuance of domain-name-removal orders after nothing more than summary ex parte proceedings— proceedings in which only the prosecutor and the judge, and not the individual or individuals responsible for the websites' activities, are present.

What this means is that some Korean, or Brazilian, or Russian website operator wakes up one morning to discover that his domain has been "seized" by the US government, and that US ISPs are now removing it from their routing tables, and making it invisible to their subscribers. His website is still up and running—but fewer and fewer people can reach it.

Additionally, some of his credit card accounts seem to have been deactivated, the pop-up advertisements he paid for (possibly in connection with an entirely unrelated business venture) have stopped appearing, and he seems to be unable to collect the contracted-for payments for the advertisements that are appearing on his site. If he can figure out what is going on (which may be no small task, even for someone who speaks English; see note 4) he can challenge all this—perhaps on the grounds that his website is *not* "dedicated to infringing activities" at all, perhaps on the grounds that under Korean, or Brazilian, or Russian law his actions are entirely lawful, or perhaps on the grounds that the prosecutor or the complaining intellectual property rightsholder just got it wrong, as prosecutors and rightsholders sometimes do. But to do so, he'll have to come to the United States and get legal representation (if he wants to contest the court's seizure of his domain name) or navigate through the section 103(b)(5)(A) counter-notification procedures to do so, in either case subjecting himself to the personal jurisdiction of the US courts.[10]

Second, SOPA would have authorized a deeply troubling kind of "vigilante enforcement" regime: copyright holders, acting entirely on their own without the intervention even of a prosecutor or a judge or any public official, would have been able simply to provide *written notice* to banks, credit card companies, Internet search engines, and Internet advertisers regarding the allegedly infringing conduct of the foreign websites, and the recipients of such notices would then have five days to cease doing any business with the offending website or risk losing an immunity from suit for damages caused by the website's continuing operation.[11]

Imagine this scenario: A guy walks into a bank. He finds the branch manager and says the following to him: "You know Farmer Jones, whose place is just down the road from mine? He's been dumping horse manure in my pond, and spoiling it for my livestock. He's a nasty SOB. Stop doing business with him. Freeze his account."

In our realspace legal world, the bank will (and should) refuse. "We're sorry, but we can't take your word for it," it will say; "bring us a court order and we'll comply, but we're not going to deny Farmer Jones access to our services just because *you* think he's acting illegally."

More to the point, in a world where the due process of law is respected, the law surely does not and cannot *compel* the bank to comply with the demand, or offer it a reward for doing so—precisely what SOPA would have done.

SOPA IS UNWORKABLE AND UNJUST

It's not just that SOPA seems to have been drawn from some bad cyberpunk novel; it is, I would suggest, both unworkable and, much more importantly, unjust. It is unworkable because the network architecture virtually guarantees that evasion will be widespread and rather simple to accomplish: tools that allow websites to instantaneously alter their domain names and redirect traffic to the new sites without any special action on a user's part are already widely available, and will surely become more so if this approach becomes commonplace. SOPA would *not* stamp out copyright infringement on the Internet; it probably wouldn't even make much of a *dent* in copyright infringement. If there are 50,000 pirate websites out there and SOPA somehow managed to close half of them down, that still leaves you with 25,000 bad guys. And in the world of bits—where information is infinitely reproducible at virtually no cost—25,000 bad guys can do just as much damage to your intellectual property as 50,000 bad guys.

And SOPA is unjust because one of the very small number of truly fundamental principles undergirding our legal system, and the rule of law itself, enshrined (twice!) in our Constitution, is that you may not deprive anyone of life, liberty, or property without due process of law: a *meaningful opportunity* to be heard, before a neutral magistrate, in an adversarial proceeding in which one gets to present one's own side of the story, in a forum that can lawfully assert jurisdiction over one or one's property.

"Stop exaggerating!" SOPA supporters might say. "We've had a 'notice and takedown' scheme in our copyright law for the last decade and a half,[12] and it has worked pretty well without any complaints about depriving people of their due process rights. SOPA just extends that scheme to offshore sites not otherwise subject to (or compliant with) US law. Why all the fuss?"

It's true: we do indeed have a notice-and-takedown scheme in the Copyright Act, under which website owners or operators are given a reward (in the form of statutory immunity from infringement liability) if they "respond expeditiously [to] remove or disable access to" allegedly infringing content upon receipt of a copyright holder's notification that the content in question is infringing. And it's also true that the Digital Millennium Copyright Act notice-and-takedown scheme has worked quite well, removing immense quantities of infringing material from distribution over the Internet while imposing few burdens on user expression or the free flow of information.[13]

But SOPA is hardly notice-and-takedown; it's more like notice-and-destroy. SOPA wouldn't "take down" *any* infringing content at all—it would take down the purveyor of the content, the person or entity supposedly responsible for the supposedly infringing distribution. It is one thing to say, as the DMCA does, that website operators have the responsibility to "remove or disable access to" content *they are making available on the Internet* once a copyright holder has identified the content as infringing; it is quite another to say that once a copyright holder has identified you as an infringer we will proceed to banish you, to make you invisible—invisible to the Internet routers, and invisible to the entire commercial infrastructure (credit card companies, advertisers, etc.) on which your continued survival may well depend.

"Well," SOPA supporters might counter, "if you don't like the notice-and-takedown analogy, how about the Customs Service? SOPA puts up a cyber-wall around US territory in order to prevent persons operating *outside* US borders from entering and bringing unlawful material—contraband movies and handbags—with them. Customs agents board and search ships at the US borders all the time, and if they find 100,000 DVD copies of *Avatar* in the hold, they seize those copies and ultimately destroy them, and nobody screams 'due process' when this happens. SOPA is just like that."

Except it isn't. The Customs Service analogy doesn't work; there are no ships, and there are no borders, no "French" or "Brazilian" or "American" parts of the Internet, but a single global network. We can try to impose borders onto it, through legislative enactments like SOPA, that create an "American" portion of the Internet and encourage the Brazilians to construct a "Brazilian" portion of the

Internet, and the Australians to construct an "Australian" portion, and so on; *but why on earth would we want to do that?* Why would we want the Internet to look like the map of the world in 1950 or 1975 or 2005? What gives the net its extraordinary and transformative power (see "Spring, Arab") is precisely the fact that it has no borders, that it is a single global network that connects everyone as peers. We already have thousands upon thousands of little internets—the world is full of those. But we have only one Internet. Chopping it up into pieces would destroy it.

It's not just that SOPA would run roughshod over the principle of due process—though it would.[14] It is the argument that we don't have to provide due process here because we're just "seizing property" located "inside" United States borders; and in any event, we needn't worry that SOPA might violate the due process rights of foreign website owners *because as foreign nationals standing outside US borders, they don't have due process rights.* As the Supreme Court put it, "Aliens receive constitutional protections [only] when they have come within the territory of the United States and developed substantial connections with this country."[15]

While we are perhaps not *required* to provide due process to those residing outside our borders, that hardly means that we shouldn't do so. The Constitution of the United States, remember, doesn't bestow the right to due process upon us; it declares that the government *won't deprive us of the due process rights we all already have* by virtue of the fact that we are human beings. *That* is the principle on which we should begin building a just, legal regime for our new global place.

Copyrighted works are important, culturally and economically, and they are worth protecting. They are not, however, sacred objects that we should protect at any cost. The damage SOPA would have done to the technical and legal infrastructure of the net is immense, and its benefits would have been negligible. RIP, SOPA. May your sleep be long and untroubled, and may you not rise, as I fear you will, from your grave to haunt us again any time soon.

1. Larry Downes, "The Revolt against Congress's New Internet Piracy Proposals," *Forbes*, November 28, 2011, http://www.forbes.com/sites /larrydownes/2011/11/28/the-revolt-against-congresss-new-internet -piracy-proposals/.

2. SOPA (the Stop Online Piracy Act) was only one of the cleverly acronymed bills advancing through Congress last year to deal with online infringement; others included PIPA (the Protect IP Act), COICA (the Combating Online Infringement and Counterfeits Act), and the magnificently named E-Parasite Act—"Enforcing and Protecting American Rights Against Sites Intent on Theft and Exploitation." I will use "SOPA" as a generic descriptor of this class of bills throughout this article, referring to the last of the bills, H.R. 3261, available online at http://www.govtrack.us/congress/bills/112/hr3261/text, as illustrative of the entire class.

3. Among its other flaws, SOPA was damned near incomprehensible. We have, I suppose, gotten used to Copyright Act amendments that, like SOPA, run to 78 pages of mind-numbing prose, but we should not pass over the matter without comment. Madison recognized the danger of this strategy 225 years ago:

> It poisons the blessings of liberty itself [and] will be of little avail to the people that the laws are made by men of their own choice, if the laws be so voluminous that they cannot be read, or so incoherent that they cannot be understood . . . . Law is defined to be a rule of action; but how can that be a rule which is little known and less fixed? [This gives] unreasonable advantage to the sagacious, the enterprising, and the moneyed few, over the industrious and uninformed mass of the people. Every new regulation concerning commerce or revenue, or in any manner affecting the value of the different species of property, presents a new harvest to those who watch the change, and can trace its consequences; a harvest reared not by themselves but by the toils and cares of the great body of their fellow citizens.

This is a state of things in which it may be said with some truth that laws are made for the *few* not for the *many*. (*The Federalist* No. 62.)

Here, for example, is how one figures out the meaning of "foreign infringing site" (to which many of the statute's provisions are specifically directed). A "foreign infringing site" must be, first, a "foreign Internet site," SOPA § 102(a)(1), defined as "an Internet site that is not a domestic Internet site." SOPA § 101(8). A "domestic Internet site" is "an Internet site for which the corresponding domain name . . . is a domestic domain name." SOPA § 101(5). A "domestic domain name" is "a domain name that is registered or assigned by a domain name registrar, domain name registry, or other domain name registration authority, that is located within a judicial district of the United States." SOPA § 101(3).

So it's a foreign Internet site if it operates under a domain name that is *not* registered by a domain name registry or registrar located in the US. A foreign Internet site is a "foreign *infringing* site" if it is, first, a "U.S.-directed site." SOPA § 102(a). US-directed site means

an Internet site or portion thereof that is used to conduct business directed to residents of the United States, or that otherwise demonstrates the existence of minimum contacts sufficient for the exercise of personal jurisdiction over the owner or operator of the Internet site consistent with the Constitution of the United States, based on relevant evidence that may include whether

(A) the Internet site is used to provide goods or services to users located in the United States;
(B) there is evidence that the Internet site or portion thereof is intended to offer or provide
(i) such goods and services,
(ii) access to such goods and services, or
(iii) delivery of such goods and services,
to users located in the United States;

(C) the Internet site or portion thereof does not contain reasonable measures to prevent such goods and services from being obtained in or delivered to the United States; and
(D) any prices for goods and services are indicated or billed in the currency of the United States.
(SOPA § 101[8].)

A U.S.-directed site is a foreign infringing site if "the owner or operator of such Internet site is committing or facilitating the commission of criminal violations punishable under [specific sections of the U.S. Code, including the Copyright and Trademark Acts]," SOPA § 102(a)(2), and the Internet site would "be subject to seizure in the United States in an action brought by the Attorney General if such site were a 'domestic Internet site.'" SOPA § 102(a)(3).

4. SOPA § 102(b).
5. Ibid.
6. SOPA § 102(c)(2)(A).
7. For a more detailed overview of how those routing tables work or how Internet message routing works more generally, see chapter 10 ("Governing Cyberspace II: Names") of my book *In Search of Jefferson's Moose: Notes on the State of Cyberspace*.
8. Steve Crocker, David Dagon, Dan Kaminsky, Danny McPherson, and Paul Vixie, "Security and Other Technical Concerns Raised by the DNS Filtering Requirements in the PROTECT IP Bill" (May 2011), http://domainincite.com/docs/PROTECT-IP-Technical-Whitepaper-Final.pdf. Several of the authors were instrumental in the current design of the DNS, and continue to operate critical portions of the DNS infrastructure.
9. Victoria Espinel, Aneesh Chopra, and Howard Schmidt, "Combating Online Piracy While Protecting an Open and Innovative Internet" (Official White House Response to two petitions concerning SOPA and the E-Parasite Act), accessed October 12, 2012, https://wwws.whitehouse.gov/petition-tool/response/combating-online-piracy-while-protecting-open-and-innovative-internet.
10. Keep in mind, when contemplating what a SOPA-enabled world might

look like, that the United States is of course not the only country that can take these steps: France, and Brazil, and Thailand, and many other countries, could try to remedy *their* rightsholders' injuries (as measured by their local laws) by deleting domains, canceling credit card accounts, and the like.

11. See SOPA § 103(b). This obligation is waived only if the owner of the domain name in question submits a "counter-notification" to the ISP, bank, credit card company, search engine, or Internet ad network, in the form prescribed by section 103(b)(5)(A) of the statute. That provision, in turn, requires the counter-notifier—the owner or operator of the website in question—to declare (a) that he or she "consents to the jurisdiction of the courts of the United States," and (b) that he or she "has a good faith belief that [the site] does not meet the criteria of an 'Internet site dedicated to theft of U.S. property.'" (As to how he or she would figure that out, see note 3—keeping in mind that the counter-notifier is quite likely to have a limited command of English.)

Maybe it's just me, but this has an Orwellian, nightmarish cast to it—all these account suspensions and counter-suspensions, domain deletion orders, notifications and counter-notifications, flowing through the network in possibly enormous numbers. Although it is impossible to know how many sites would have been subject to SOPA seizure orders or notifications, the number would likely have been immense. Internet scale is unprecedented—as my colleague James Grimmelmann put it, "The Internet is sublimely large; in comparison to it, all other human activity is small." James Grimmelmann, "The Internet Is a Semicommons," *Fordham Law Review* 78, no. 6 (2010): 2803. The "notice-and-takedown" procedure implemented in US copyright law by the 1998 Digital Millennium Copyright Act, on which SOPA was purportedly modeled (see note 14), can perhaps give us some idea of the potential scale and scope of SOPA notification. While it is impossible to accurately ascertain the total number of DMCA takedown notices that have been issued since enactment of the DMCA, Google Inc. estimated that during 2010 it disabled access to approximately 3 million URLs pursuant to DMCA takedown notices. See Google Comments to the Department of Commerce, "Inquiry on Copyright

Policy, Creativity, and Innovation in the Internet Economy," Docket No. 100910448-0448-01, accessed October 12, 2012, http://www.ntia.doc .gov/comments/100910448-0448-01/comment.cfm?e=6BDC88CD -BD11-4506-9196-220C54FBBB87. See also Viacom Int'l Inc. v. You-Tube, Inc., 718 F. Supp. 2d 514, 524 (S.D.N.Y. 2010)—noting that a single website (YouTube) received more than 100,000 takedown notices from a single copyright holder (Viacom Inc.) on February 2, 2007.

12. SOPA's notification-and-counter-notification scheme was, as those of you who are familiar with US copyright law might have already surmised, modeled on the "notice and takedown" copyright enforcement scheme enacted in 1998 in section 512 of the Digital Millennium Copyright Act, 17 U.S.C. § 512(c). For those of you unfamiliar with notice-and-takedown, it works more or less as follows. Under the DMCA, once a copyright holder notifies a website operator that his or her copyright-protected work "resides on a system or network controlled by or operated by or for" the website operator, the operator must "respond expeditiously" to "remove, or disable access to, the material that is claimed to be infringing," unless there is counter-notification from the party responsible for the allegedly infringing posting; if the website operator does so, it obtains a "safe harbor" from any liability for the infringement.

13. In an amicus brief submitted to the Court of Appeals for the Second Circuit in the recently concluded *Viacom v. YouTube* appeal (available online at http://www.scribd.com/doc/109867487), I wrote (with coauthor Annemarie Bridy, and on behalf of 43 signatory law professors):

> Over the last decade, the scheme that Congress implemented in the DMCA . . . has been resoundingly, and perhaps even remarkably, successful at forging an equitable balance among [copyright holders and users]. Website operators and other providers of innovative online services have a clear and straightforward set of ground rules to follow, allowing them to conform their operations to the law and, thereby, to avoid the specter of potentially crushing liability. At the same time, copyright holders, through the notice-and-takedown process

spelled out in 17 U.S.C. § 512(c), have simple and cost-effective means to curtail large numbers of unauthorized and infringing uses of their protected expression.

The benefits that Internet users—i.e., the public—have reaped from this compromise have been profound. The DMCA has fueled extraordinary and unprecedented growth in innovative Internet services based entirely on user expression. This explosion of *participatory* (often referred to as "user-generated content," or "Web 2.0") online services and applications has, in turn, fueled the growth and evolution of the Internet itself as a truly global communications platform, one that has become, as the daily news headlines continue to remind us, a powerful tool for grassroots democratic movements around the world. Thousands of Internet businesses, many of which are now household names across the globe—e.g., Facebook, Twitter, YouTube, Blogger, Craigslist, MySpace, Tumblr, Flickr, and many, many others—have emerged over the past decade sharing one common characteristic: they provide virtually no content of their own (copyrightable or otherwise), but rely instead entirely on their users to make the sites valuable, engaging, and attractive for other users. Internet users have responded in truly breathtaking numbers. It is difficult, if not impossible, to imagine this development in the absence of strong DMCA safe harbors.

At the same time, the DMCA safe harbors provide copyright holders with a direct, efficient, and effective remedy against infringing conduct on the massive scale made possible by participatory media platforms. Through the notice-and-takedown procedures set forth in § 512(c), hundreds of thousands, or perhaps millions, of infringing works have been quickly removed from circulation over the Internet through a process that avoids costly and time-consuming adjudication while simultaneously providing due consideration of the interests of all parties involved.

14. I'm not aware of any SOPA supporter who argues that SOPA actually *does* provide foreign website operators with a meaningful opportunity to be heard, before a neutral magistrate, in an adversarial proceeding

and in a forum that can lawfully assert jurisdiction over them or their property, before depriving them of their ability to communicate with millions of Internet users in the United States.

15. United States v. Verdugo-Urquidez, 494 U.S. 259, 271 (1990).

4

How the Criminalization of Copyright Threatens Innovation and the Rule of Law

Timothy B. Lee

I N 1984, THE Supreme Court narrowly rejected Hollywood's argument that Sony should be held liable for copyright infringements by users of its Betamax VCR. Writing for the majority, Justice John Paul Stevens acknowledged that copyright holders have a "legitimate demand for effective—not merely symbolic—protection of the statutory monopoly" provided by copyright law.[1] But he concluded that the creator of a general-purpose technology with "substantial non-infringing uses" was not liable if some of its customers used the technology to infringe copyright. Many people regard the *Sony* decision as the legal foundation of the modern consumer electronics industry.

Two decades later, the high court reached the opposite conclusion about the peer-to-peer file-sharing service Grokster. A unanimous court ruled that the firm was liable because it had deliberately "induced" infringement by its users.[2] Still, some justices were concerned that an overly broad ruling could discourage future innovation. During oral arguments, Justice Stephen Breyer worried that ruling against Grokster would set a precedent that, if it had been in place five years earlier, would have made it hard for an attorney to "recommend to the iPod inventor that he could go ahead" and invent the iPod.

This trade-off between the harms of infringement and the harms to innovation from overzealous enforcement have been central to the copyright debate for decades. In *Sony*, *Grokster*, and other cases, the courts have tried to fashion a body of law that strikes a balance between these dangers.

Two related trends in copyright enforcement threaten to upend this balance. First, the federal government has begun to criminally prosecute online intermediaries who allegedly facilitate the infringing activities of users. That's a change from the traditional approach, exemplified by the *Sony* and *Grokster* cases, in which major content companies brought *civil* lawsuits against technology firms.

Second, using civil forfeiture powers granted by the 2008 PRO-IP Act, the federal government has begun seizing the domain names, servers, and other assets of online intermediaries. These seizures typically occur before the owners are convicted of any crime, and in some cases property is seized without its owners ever being charged.

These trends threaten to transform copyright law, making the legal precedents the courts have developed in recent decades practically irrelevant. When an entrepreneur faces a civil lawsuit, the worst that can happen is that his firm will be forced into bankruptcy. In contrast, a criminal case can mean jail time for a firm's executives.

The complexity and novelty of online copyright cases means that the law is often unsettled. So executives facing criminal penalties have a strong incentive to accept a plea bargain even if they believe they have acted lawfully. But while that may be rational for an individual defendant, it deprives the courts of an opportunity to establish a precedent that could make the law more predictable in the future.

Even more troubling, the threat of criminal prosecutions could cause online service providers to give a wide berth to business models that could be construed as piracy-promoting, even if they could bring significant consumer benefits. After all, the first VCRs, the first MP3 players, and YouTube all faced civil lawsuits from major copyright holders when they were introduced. If the creator of the next great media technology has to worry about *criminal* prosecution, it will make Justice Breyer's concerns in *Grokster* look quaint by comparison.

In this chapter, I will briefly review copyright enforcement efforts brought against online intermediaries during the first decade of the 21st century. Then I'll take a detailed look at some copyright enforcement efforts undertaken since the passage of the PRO-IP Act in 2008. The former were civil lawsuits brought by private rightsholders. In contrast, the latter are undertaken by the federal government and make use of criminal prosecutions and asset forfeiture—powers not available to plaintiffs in civil lawsuits. After examining these case studies, I will argue that the criminalization of copyright infringement has gone too far.

THE PEER-TO-PEER WARS

For most of the 20th century, copyright infringement involved duplicating physical media such as books, cassette tapes, or DVDs. The significant economies of scale to physical content distribution resulted in two distinct types of piracy: large-scale commercial piracy and casual amateur sharing. Because the latter had only a modest effect on the market for copyrighted works, antipiracy efforts focused primarily on the former.

The Internet radically reduced the cost of making and distributing unauthorized copies of copyrighted works, erasing the previously clear line between commercial piracy and amateur sharing. Suddenly, millions of ordinary people had the ability to distribute copyrighted works to strangers around the world with minimal effort and at negligible cost.

It would have been logistically impossible to sue or prosecute every direct infringer, so major content companies began targeting intermediaries—online services that help users to find and share information with each other. In December 1999, major record labels sued Napster, an early "peer to peer" file-sharing site.[3] Napster provided users with the ability to offer files for others to download and a search engine to help users find music they wanted. But Napster employees did not actively review or approve files made available on the Napster network. Napster argued that this fact shielded it from liability for its users' infringing activities. But the company lost its court battle and was forced to shut down the service in 2001.[4]

In the decade since Napster's demise, a variety of other intermediaries have sprung up to take its place. And many of them have faced their own lawsuits from major content companies. We've already mentioned the *Grokster* fight, which went all the way to the Supreme Court in 2005. Grokster had a more decentralized architecture than Napster; information about which files users were sharing never passed through Grokster's servers. Grokster argued that this architectural decision shielded it from liability. But the high court found Grokster liable because it had actively encouraged ("induced") the use of its service for illicit purposes.[5] Hollywood's victory over Grokster forced several other peer-to-peer services, including Morpheus,[6] eDonkey,[7] and Kazaa,[8] to shut down as well.

Content industries' impressive winning streak against commercial peer-to-peer companies caused many users to shift to open file-sharing protocols that were not under the control of any specific company. One of these, the BitTorrent protocol, is now the leading peer-to-peer platform.

BitTorrent is an efficient system for distributing digital content, but it lacks a built-in mechanism for searching or browsing available files. A variety of BitTorrent search engines and directories arose to meet this need, and content companies began suing those as well. For example, the Motion Picture Association of America sued a BitTorrent search engine called ISOHunt in 2006,[9] leading to an injunction against the site.[10]

THE RISE OF LOCKER SITES

At the same time they were suing intermediaries, some content companies were also suing individual users.[11] The fear of such lawsuits has spurred the emergence of an alternate file-sharing model. It consists of two distinct types of intermediaries: link sites and locker sites. Locker sites offer the capacity to make files available to the public, but they typically preserve plausible deniability by omitting any way to browse or search the files available on the site. Link sites provide this missing functionality, offering organized directories of content available for download from various locker sites.

This division of labor has proven popular among those seeking to profit from illicit file-sharing because it gives each type of site a plausible legal defense. Locker sites compare themselves to the video-sharing site YouTube and the file-storage service DropBbox. Users sometimes use these mainstream products to share works in violation of copyright law, but the companies providing the services enjoy a robust "safe harbor" against liability under the 1998 Digital Millennium Copyright Act. Locker sites argue they are eligible for the same safe harbor.

For their part, link sites emphasize that they merely offer pointers to other sites' content, and do not host files themselves. Indeed, courts in the United Kingdom and Spain have upheld the legality of some link sites.

Like Napster and Grokster before them, these intermediaries have faced lawsuits from major content companies. For example, the Motion Picture Association of America sued the locker site Hotfile for copyright infringement in February 2011.[12]

"ROGUE SITES"

All of the legal disputes we've discussed so far have one thing in common: they were civil lawsuits initiated by private firms. For more than a decade, companies like Napster, Grokster, YouTube, ISOHunt, and Hotfile have had to worry that lawsuits by major content companies could drive them into bankruptcy. But until recently, entrepreneurs building cutting-edge media technologies didn't need to worry that prosecution by the federal government could lead to lengthy prison sentences for their executives. Nor did they have to worry that the federal government might seize their domain names, servers, and other property, effectively shutting them down before they've had their day in court.

Indeed, copyright infringement was no more than a misdemeanor offense until 1976. But lobbying by major content companies produced a series of bills—passed in 1976, 1982, 1992, and 1996—that beefed up criminal penalties for a wide variety of copyright violations. Many more infringements became eligible for criminal prosecution. The maximum fine increased from $1,000 in 1975 to $250,000 today. The maximum prison term rose from one year to five years.[13] In 1997, Congress passed the No Electronic Theft Act, which extended criminal penalties to noncommercial infringers.

Still, law enforcement agencies have better things to do than prosecute college kids for swapping movies on BitTorrent, so until recently the government exercised these powers relatively sparingly.

All that changed about five years ago when Hollywood and the major labels began seeking the active participation of the federal government in their campaign against online intermediaries. They secured the passage of the PRO-IP Act in 2008. It expanded the use of civil asset forfeiture in copyright cases, allowing the seizure of not only infringing copies themselves, but also "any property used, or intended to be used" to commit copyright infringement, as well as "any property constituting or derived from any proceeds obtained directly or indirectly as a result."[14]

Major content companies began using the phrase "rogue site" to describe locker and link sites. They argued that the "rogue site" problem required Congress to pass legislation like the Stop Online Piracy Act. They simultaneously pressed law enforcement officials to use powers they already had, including the forfeiture powers of the PRO-IP Act, to combat rogue sites.

As we saw in chapter 3, Congress rebuffed requests to enact SOPA. But the Obama administration was more receptive to calls for increased enforcement. In 2010, Immigration and Customs Enforcement began Operation In Our Sites, a project to use the government's power of civil asset forfeiture to seize domains belonging to sites allegedly guilty of copyright or trademark infringement. Between June 2010 and November 2011, the government seized 350 domains.[15] As of November 2011, 116 of those domains had been forfeited to the government. The government has also brought criminal charges against the operators of some locker sites and link sites.

Next we will examine some of these government enforcement efforts in detail. To be clear, most of the sites the government has targeted so far really do seem to have profited from the infringing activities of their users. (As we'll see, the seizure of dajaz1.com appears to have been a simple mistake.) If they were based in the United States, these sites would likely be vulnerable to a lawsuit under the *Grokster* inducement standard.

But it's less clear whether the operators of sites based overseas have broken the law in their own countries. And there's also doubt about whether their actions constitute criminal offenses under US law. More importantly, even apparently culpable defendants deserve to be treated as innocent until proven guilty. As we will see, the government's new, more aggressive enforcement posture has imposed significant harm on many of its targets long before they have had their day in court.

DAJAZ1.COM AND ROJADIRECTA.COM

Civil asset forfeiture law is based on the legal fiction that the targeted property—not its owner—is guilty of a crime. Judges often sign off on seizure orders without giving the owner of the target property the opportunity to rebut the government's accusations.

Unsurprisingly, this can lead to errors. Take the case of dajaz1 .com, the domain of a popular hip-hop blog that was seized by the federal government in December 2010. The operator of the site, a Queens man named Andre Nasib, told the *New York Times* that his blog was popular enough that representatives of hip-hop labels and artists would sometimes leak prerelease copies of upcoming music to him in an effort to generate buzz.[16] Some of these leaked tracks were then cited in the government's seizure application as evidence of infringement.[17]

Nasib filed for the return of his domain in early 2011. But instead of either returning the domain or beginning formal forfeiture proceedings, the government applied for three consecutive 60-day extensions. The government sought the delays in part because it was waiting for the Recording Industry Association of America to answer "outstanding questions" about the domain. Evidently, the government never received a satisfactory response to these questions, and it finally returned the domain without explanation or apology in December 2011.[18] The government's mistakes—and the lack of an effective mechanism for challenging those mistakes in court—kept Nasib's website offline for a full year.

Another example involves the domain rojadirecta.com, which was a link site based in Spain. It provided sports fans with a convenient way to find video coverage of soccer games. Many of the videos allegedly infringe the copyright of professional soccer leagues, but courts in Spain have upheld the site's legality, ruling that linking to infringing videos is not itself an infringement of copyright.[19] Nevertheless, the US federal government seized the domain in early 2011. After months of fruitless efforts to get it back, in June 2011 the owners filed a lawsuit seeking the domain's return.[20] Finally, in August 2012, the government returned the domain without explanation or apology. Once again, the government was able to hold a domain for 18 months without having to prove that its owner committed any crime.

Property rights activists have long decried the abuse of civil asset forfeiture in drug cases.[21] Civil asset forfeiture allows the government to deprive people of their property without an adversarial hearing. And it shifts the burden of proof to the property owner, effectively asking him to prove his own innocence.

But the seizure of domain names has constitutional defects that go beyond those of traditional asset seizures. Websites are platforms for speech. The Supreme Court has held that prior restraint—censorship prior to publication—violates the First Amendment.[22]

It's hard to imagine a more clear-cut example of prior restraint than the government seizing the domain of an online publication—prior to any adversarial hearing—and holding it for months.

Such seizures are also inconsistent with the Supreme Court's interpretation of the Fifth Amendment. In 1974, the high court upheld the government's seizure of a yacht because it was the kind of property "that could be removed to another jurisdiction, destroyed, or concealed, if advance warning of confiscation were given."[23] But the court has ruled that the same reasoning does *not* apply to real property. Land and buildings cannot easily be moved, concealed, or destroyed, the Supreme Court ruled in 1993, so "the Due Process Clause requires the Government to afford notice and a meaningful opportunity to be heard before seizing real property subject to civil forfeiture."[24]

Exactly the same reasoning applies to domain seizures. A domain name is simply an entry in a database. Operation In Our Sites focused on domain names, such as .org and .com, for which the relevant databases are controlled by third parties subject to US jurisdiction. Therefore, it will always be possible to order that a domain be transferred to the government after its owner has had his day in court. That means the government is obligated to afford domain owners due process *before* seizing their domains.

NINJAVIDEO AND TV SHACK

In 2011, the government began criminally prosecuting the operators of some of the websites whose domains it had previously seized. A site called NinjaVideo was one of the first targets. Its lead administrator, Hana Beshara, and four others were charged with criminal copyright infringement in September. Beshara and her associates pled guilty. Beshara was sentenced to two years in prison.

Beshara understood that users were drawn to her site largely because it offered links to infringing copies of copyrighted movies and TV shows. She expected to eventually face a civil lawsuit, though she says she believed—implausibly—that she was eligible for the "safe harbor" provided by the 1998 Digital Millennium Copyright Act. However, Beshara told the *American Prospect* in 2011 that "we never thought they would come after us like criminals."[25]

That wasn't a crazy supposition. There don't appear to have been any criminal prosecutions of sites like NinjaVideo in the United States before 2011. It's well established that online services can face civil liability for facilitating the infringing activities of their users, but the contours of such "secondary" copyright liability have been fleshed out by the courts rather than Congress. And generally speaking, criminal offenses must be explicitly defined by Congress. So it's unclear whether operating a link site can constitute a criminal offense under American law.

Given the uncertainty of her legal position, Beshara's decision to accept a two-year plea bargain may have been personally rational. But because her case didn't go to trial, the boundaries of criminal copyright infringement will remain murky for future defendants.

Also indicted in 2011 was Richard O'Dwyer, a British college student who operated a link site called TV Shack. Rather than prosecuting him in the United Kingdom, American and British authorities have sought O'Dwyer's extradition to the United States. That decision was made despite the fact that neither O'Dwyer nor his servers have been located in the United States since TV Shack was created. It's also not clear that O'Dwyer has broken British law. A British judge upheld the legality of a similar site, called TV-Links, in 2010.[26]

In an interview with *Ars Technica*, O'Dwyer's mother, Julia, said that facing trial in the United States would be a hardship for Richard and his family. He would be cut off from his friends and family and unable to continue his studies or seek employment. According to Julia O'Dwyer, "It will cost £1500 [US$2,300] at least to have a trip to America. And then you go all that way for an hour's visiting time in jail." She called extradition "an extra punishment that you're given before you even get to any charges."[27]

She has a point. If Richard O'Dwyer committed a crime under British law, he ought to be tried in the United Kingdom. If British copyright laws are too lax, major copyright holders can lobby the authorities to beef them up. But the mere fact that some of the people using O'Dwyer's site were Americans shouldn't be enough to make him subject to US law. And forcing him to stand trial thousands of miles from home does seem like an unfair punishment imposed before he has been convicted of any crime.

MEGAUPLOAD

The highest-profile target of the government's campaign against online intermediaries is the locker site Megaupload and its CEO, Kim Dotcom. In 2011, Megaupload was one of the world's highest-traffic websites. It allowed users to upload large files and make them available for others to download—a capability that has many applications, both lawful and unlawful. It claimed to be responsible for 4 percent of all Internet traffic.[28] In January 2012 a coordinated international raid involving officials from the United States, New Zealand, and other countries seized the megaupload .com domain, shut down Megaupload's servers, arrested Kim Dotcom and his top executives at his residence in New Zealand, and froze all the defendants' assets.[29]

Kim Dotcom and his associates are entitled to a presumption of innocence until they are found guilty by a jury. Unfortunately, the government has adopted a range of tactics seemingly calculated to punish Dotcom and his associates before they've had their day in court.

Practically speaking, the indictment and related seizures destroyed Megaupload. Since January, its servers have been switched off, its employees have gone unpaid, and its customers—some of whom paid for premium accounts and used them to store valuable data—have not been able to use the site. Even if Dotcom ultimately prevails in court, it could take years to rebuild the site. It may even prove impossible if competitors consolidate their market positions in the meantime.

When New Zealand officials raided Kim Dotcom's home, they executed a search warrant calling for the seizure of "all digital devices, including electronic devices capable of storing and/or processing data in digital form."[30] While some of these devices presumably contained information relevant to the indictment, others contained data unrelated to the case—including personal files belonging to Dotcom and his family and surveillance video that could confirm or deny Dotcom's claims that the police used excessive force in their raid. The hard drives were transferred to the United States over the objections of the New Zealand judge overseeing Dotcom's extradition case. The same judge has ruled that the search warrant was so broad as to be invalid under New Zealand law.[31] As of August 2012, the government has refused Dotcom's request for copies of his files to help prepare for a forthcoming extradition hearing; litigation on that issue is ongoing.

The government has also impeded efforts by Dotcom and his associates to obtain legal representation. All funds belonging to Dotcom, his codefendants, and the Megaupload corporation were frozen at the time of the raid. Megaupload and Dotcom sought to have enough funds unfrozen to cover their legal bills. The government has argued that Dotcom should pay his lawyers using funds that were released by the New Zealand courts—though Dotcom notes that these funds have been specifically earmarked for living expenses, not legal bills. The government has opposed the release of *any* funds to pay for the defense of Megaupload, which is legally a distinct entity entitled to its own representation.

By freezing Megaupload's assets, the government also placed the data on Megaupload's servers—including the data of thousands of Megaupload users, some of whom were using the site in noninfringing ways—in jeopardy. Megaupload leased 1,103 servers from Carpathia Hosting in Virginia. When Megaupload's bank accounts were frozen, it became unable to pay its bills. In March, Carpathia told the court that keeping the servers idle was costing the company thousands of dollars per day. It warned that if those bills are not paid, Carpathia could be forced to delete the data so that it can reallocate the servers for use by other customers.

Megaupload wants to pay Carpathia for the servers in order to preserve its customers' data. But the government has objected to this arrangement, arguing that Megaupload's funds are the proceeds of illegal activities and that the data on the servers are contraband. But of course the government has not yet proven these claims to a jury. And not only could deleting the 25 petabytes of data on the Megaupload servers do irreparable harm to Megaupload's business, it could also destroy evidence Megaupload needs to mount an effective legal defense.

In short, the government's power to seize assets prior to conviction is making a mockery of Kim Dotcom's constitutional rights. He has the right to a presumption of innocence, but his business has been effectively destroyed before he sets foot inside a courtroom. He has a right to counsel, but the government has effectively prevented him from paying his legal bills with his own funds. He has a right to exculpatory evidence, but the government is refusing to give him copies of data it seized from his home and has shown little concern that its actions could result in the destruction of evidence on the Megaupload servers.

DECRIMINALIZING COPYRIGHT

It's useful to step back and ask whether it makes sense to criminalize copyright infringement in the first place. Crimes like murder, rape, and arson do grave injustices to their victims, and we want to create the strongest possible deterrent.

The argument for criminalizing copyright infringement is less clear-cut. The Constitution authorizes copyrights in order to "promote the progress of science and the useful arts."[32] That utilitarian justification suggests that we should take a pragmatic approach to copyright enforcement. It's important to provide enough copyright protection to stimulate the production of creative works. But copyright infringement is not such a grave injustice that it needs to be stamped out at any cost.

Users determined to flout the law will always be able to find infringing works in the seedy corners of the Internet. But most users prefer the convenience, quality, and clean conscience of obtaining content from legitimate vendors. So the copyright system doesn't need to eliminate piracy altogether; it merely needs to make infringing sites sufficiently unprofitable and marginal that licensed services can thrive.

The pre-2010 enforcement regime, with its reliance on civil lawsuits rather than criminal penalties, appears to have achieved this goal. To be sure, such lawsuits did not eliminate piracy from the Internet altogether. But legitimate services like iTunes and Netflix prospered during the first decade of the 21st century. And perhaps as a consequence, the market continued to produce an abundance of creative works.[33]

At the same time, criminalization has significant costs, and these costs are particularly high when online intermediaries—as opposed to those who directly infringe copyright—are targeted.

The distinction between an innovative online media service and a rogue site can be rather subtle. Consider Megaupload and YouTube. Both store and redistribute creative works submitted by users. Both claim to comply with the "notice and takedown" regime specified by the Digital Millennium Copyright Act. Both offer cash payments to the uploaders of popular content.

And both have non-infringing uses. For example, the Electronic Frontier Foundation is representing Kyle Goodwin, an Ohio videographer who used Megaupload as a backup service for his videos. Goodwin experienced a hard drive crash shortly before Megaupload was shut down. As a result, the Carpathia servers hold the only remaining copies of his commercially valuable videos.

This isn't to say that Megaupload is necessarily a legitimate business and Kim Dotcom an innocent victim. But the exact line between an infringing file-sharing service and a legitimate cloud storage service is far from clear. Cloud storage services are the latest in a long list of once cutting-edge technologies, including the VCR, MP3 players, cloud music services, book search engines, and online video sites, that have faced accusations of copyright infringement. Most of these innovations eventually prevailed in court. But it wasn't obvious ex ante that they would prevail. And society benefitted from the fact that entrepreneurs in each of these categories were willing to push forward despite the legal risks.

A particularly poignant example is the case of My.MP3.com, a precursor of modern cloud music services like Google Play and Amazon Cloud Player. Launched by entrepreneur Michael Robertson at the turn of the century as part of his company MP3.com, it was not a file-sharing service. It merely allowed users to upload music from CDs they already owned so that they could listen to their music from other Internet-connected computers. But to cope with the limited bandwidth of its day, the company took what proved to be a fatal shortcut. Rather than requiring users to upload the entire contents of a CD, it took a "fingerprint" and then instantly stocked the user's online locker with music previously ripped from MP3 .com's own copy of the same CD. A district court judge found that the service infringed copyright law, forcing it to shut down. The decision may have set back the introduction of cloud music services by a decade; Amazon and Google finally entered the market in 2011.

The threat of civil liability already gives entrepreneurs strong incentives to follow the law. Adding criminal penalties may cause them to become excessively risk-averse, depriving consumers of valuable innovations. The founders of YouTube might have thought twice about launching a video website in a world where Napster founder Shawn Fanning and MP3.com founder Michael Robertson were serving prison sentences for criminal copyright infringement. We might have somewhat less piracy in that world, but we'd also have a lot less innovation in digital media technologies.

Indeed, there are already signs that the prosecution of Megaupload is causing more mainstream file-hosting services to curtail their functionality. A few days after the Megaupload raid, two file-hosting services, FileSonic and Fileserve, disabled the file-sharing feature of their sites.[34] Of course, major content companies would applaud these decisions. But such functionality has legitimate as well as illegitimate uses. Its legality ought to be determined by a judge after hearing arguments for both sides. The threat of criminal prosecution has short-circuited that process.

The rapid pace of technological progress means that the line between legitimate and illegitimate online intermediaries—between the YouTubes and the Groksters—is likely to be a fine one for the foreseeable future. That makes it all the more critical that copyright law be developed incrementally through the case-by-case adjudication of civil lawsuits. Supreme Court rulings like *Sony* and *Grokster* made the law more predictable by giving future entrepreneurs notice of what the law requires. In contrast, when copyright enforcement is done by asset seizures and criminal prosecutions, the rule of law becomes irrelevant, since prosecutors can destroy the target business long before the case reaches trial.

Criminal prosecutions of online intermediaries, and especially the seizure of assets prior to conviction, threaten the rule of law and online innovation. Congress should repeal the asset-forfeiture provisions of the PRO-IP Act and revise copyright law to make it clear that only direct copyright infringement—not the operation of a site used for infringement by users—can result in criminal sanctions.

NOTES

1. Sony Corp. of America v. Universal City Studios, 464 U.S. 417 (1984).
2. MGM Studios, Inc. v. Grokster, Ltd. 545 U.S. 913 (2005).
3. Matt Richtel, "The Napster Decision: The Overview; Appellate Judges Back Limitations on Copying Music," *New York Times*, February 13, 2001, http://www.nytimes.com/2001/02/13/business/napster -decision-overview-appellate-judges-back-limitations-copying -music.html.
4. Andrew Zipern, "Internet: Napster Suspends Service During 'Upgrade,'" *New York Times*, July 3, 2001, http://www.nytimes .com/2001/07/03/business/technology-briefing-internet-napster

-suspends-service-during-upgrade.html.

5. MGM Studios, Inc. v. Grokster, Ltd., 545 U.S. 913 (2005).

6. Eric Bangeman, "StreamCast Loses File-Sharing Suit," *Ars Technica* (blog), September 28, 2006, http://arstechnica.com /business/2006/09/7852/.

7. Nate Anderson, "No More 'Hee Haw': eDonkey Taken to the Glue Factory," *Ars Technica* (blog), September 13, 2006, http://arstechnica.com /information-technology/2006/09/7733/.

8. Eric Bangeman, "Kazaa Ponies Up to Settle with Music Publishers," *Ars Technica* (blog), November 1, 2006, http://arstechnica.com /business/2006/11/8130/.

9. Ryan Paul, "MPAA Turns Attention to USENET, Takes On Torrentspy, Isohunt, Others," *Ars Technica* (blog), February 24, 2006, http:// arstechnica.com/uncategorized/2006/02/6253-2/.

10. Nate Anderson, "1 Down, 5 to Go? IsoHunt Neutered by U.S. Judge," *Ars Technica* (blog), May 24, 2010, http://arstechnica.com /tech-policy/2010/05/1-down-5-to-go-isohunt-neutered-by-us -judge/.

11. David Kravets, "Copyright Lawsuits Plummet in Aftermath of RIAA Campaign," *Wired* (blog), May 18, 2010, http://www.wired.com /threatlevel/2010/05/riaa-bump/.

12. Jacqui Cheng, "MPAA Sues Hotfile for 'Staggering' Copyright Infringement," *Ars Technica* (blog), February 8, 2011, http://arstechnica.com /tech-policy/2011/02/mpaa-sues-hotfile-for-copyright-infringement -on-a-staggering-scale/.

13. Lydia Palla Loren, "Digitization, Commodification, Criminalization: The Evolution of Criminal Copyright Infringement and the Importance of the Willfulness Requirement," *Washington University Law Quarterly* 77 (1999): 842.

14. 18 USC § 2323.

15. United States Department of Justice, "Federal Courts Order Seizure of 150 Website Domains Involved in Selling Counterfeit Goods as Part of DOJ, ICE HSI and FBI Cyber Monday Crackdown," press release, November 28, 2011, http://www.justice.gov/opa/pr/2011/November/11 -ag-1540.html.

16. Ben Sisario, "Hip-Hop Copyright Case Had Little Explanation," *New York Times*, May 12, 2012, http://www.nytimes.com/2012/05/07/business/media/hip-hop-site-dajaz1s-copyright-case-ends-in-confusion.html.

17. Mike Masnick, "More & Bigger Mistakes Discovered in Homeland Security's Domain Seizures," *Techdirt* (blog), December 22, 2010, http://www.techdirt.com/articles/20101222/02112912376/more-bigger-mistakes-discovered-homeland-securitys-domain-seizures.shtml.

18. Timothy B. Lee, "Waiting on the RIAA, Feds Held Seized Dajaz1 Domain for Months," *Ars Technica* (blog), May 4, 2012, http://arstechnica.com/tech-policy/2012/05/waiting-on-the-riaa-feds-held-seized-dajaz1-domain-for-months/.

19. "Sports Streaming / Torrent Links Site Victorious in Court," *TorrentFreak* (blog), May 10, 2010, http://torrentfreak.com/sports-streaming-torrent-links-site-victorious-in-court-100510/.

20. David Kravets, "U.S. Faces Legal Challenge to Internet-Domain Seizures," *Wired* (blog), June 13, 2011, http://www.wired.com/threatlevel/2011/06/domain-seizure-challenge/.

21. Henry Hyde, *Forfeiting Our Property Rights* (Washington, DC: Cato Institute, 1995).

22. Near v. Minnesota, 283 U.S. 697 (1931).

23. Calero Toledo v. Pearson Yacht Leasing Co., 416 U.S. 663 (1974).

24. United States v. James Daniel Good Real Property, 510 U.S. 43 (1993).

25. Rob Fischer, "A Ninja in Our Sites" (includes comments by Hana Beshara), *American Prospect*, December 15, 2011, http://prospect.org/article/ninja-our-sites.

26. "TV-Links Triumphs with Landmark E-Commerce Directive Ruling," *TorrentFreak* (blog), February 12, 2010, http://torrentfreak.com/tv-links-triumphs-with-landmark-e-commerce-directive-ruling-100212/.

27. Timothy B. Lee, "Big Content's Latest Antipiracy Weapon: Extradition" (includes comments by Julia O'Dwyer), *Ars Technica* (blog), July 21, 2011, http://arstechnica.com/tech-policy/2011/07/big-content-unveils-latest-antipiracy-weapon-extradition/.

28. David Kravets, "Feds Shutter Megaupload, Arrest Executives," *Wired*

(blog), January 19, 2012, http://www.wired.com/threatlevel/2012/01/megaupload-indicted-shuttered/.

29. Nate Anderson, "Why the Feds Smashed Megaupload," *Ars Technica* (blog), January 19, 2012, http://arstechnica.com/tech-policy/2012/01/why-the-feds-smashed-megaupload/.

30. Timothy B. Lee, "Kim Dotcom Lawyer Blasts U.S. Government's 'Pattern of Delay,'" *Ars Technica* (blog), May 25, 2012, http://arstechnica.com/tech-policy/2012/05/kim-dotcom-lawyer-blasts-us-governments-pattern-of-delay/.

31. Nate Anderson, "Mega-Victory: Kim Dotcom Search Warrants 'Invalid,' Mansion Raid 'Illegal,'" *Ars Technica* (blog), June 28, 2012, http://arstechnica.com/tech-policy/2012/06/mega-victory-kim-dotcom-search-warrants-invalid-mansion-raid-illegal/.

32. U.S. Constitution, art. 1, sec. 8.

33. Mike Masnick and Michael Ho, *The Sky Is Rising: A Detailed Look at the State of the Entertainment Industry*, white paper sponsored by the Computer and Communications Industry Association, January 2012, http://www.techdirt.com/skyrising/.

34. Ryan Paul, "FileSonic Has Disabled File Sharing in Wake of Megaupload Takedown," *Ars Technica* (blog), January 22, 2012, http://arstechnica.com/tech-policy/2012/01/filesonic-has-disabled-file-sharing-in-wake-of-megaupload-takedown/; Jon Brodkin, "More Megaupload Fallout: FileServe Shutters File-Sharing Service," *Ars Technica* (blog), January 23, 2012, http://arstechnica.com/gadgets/2012/01/more-megaupload-fallout-fileserve-shutters-file-sharing-service/.

5

Free Expression under the DMCA

Christina Mulligan

I N MID-JULY 2012, a Mitt Romney campaign ad hosted on You-Tube was forcibly removed from the site, over the protests of the Romney campaign.[1] The removal resembled a similar incident that occurred in 2008, when YouTube blocked several John Mc-Cain ads for more than 10 days, despite the McCain campaign's pleas that YouTube put the ads back up.[2]

In both cases, YouTube removed the ads in response to claims that they violated someone's copyright. Under the Digital Millennium Copyright Act, YouTube can be held liable for copyright infringement if it doesn't remove videos upon notification that someone believes the video infringes his or her copyright. Therefore, YouTube has a very strong business interest in immediately taking down anything someone claims is copyright-infringing.

The Romney ad featured news headlines claiming President Barack Obama rewarded campaign donors and lobbyists with political positions, access to political leaders, and stimulus funds. In the background, it played a sound clip of Obama singing a single line from Al Green's song "Let's Stay Together": "I'm so in love with you." Music publisher BMG had the ad removed because it claimed the clip of Obama singing Green's song violated its copyright.[3] Four years earlier, the McCain campaign ads had been removed because they incorporated news clips from CBS, Fox, NBC, and the Christian Broadcasting Network.[4]

The Romney and McCain ads were not actually copyright-infringing. Indeed, the inclusion of President Obama's singing and the news clips qualify as "fair uses"[5] of copyrighted works under the Copyright Act—meaning that Romney's and McCain's campaigns didn't need the copyright holder's permission to use the clips. Their videos weren't illegal—yet YouTube still censored the ads for several days.

The campaign ad debacles illustrate just one of the problems with the Digital Millennium Copyright Act, but there are many others. This chapter explores a few of them. The first section explains what the DMCA does and how it works. The second describes the DMCA's effects on competition and on fair uses of copyrighted works. The third situates the DMCA in the history of liberty of the press, and the final section discusses how the DMCA chills freedom of expression.

STRUCTURE OF THE DMCA

Understanding how the DMCA threatens free expression and free competition requires a quick overview of the law. The DMCA has two primary parts: the anticircumvention provisions and the safe harbors for Internet and online service providers, which will be considered in turn.[6]

The anticircumvention provisions concern the legal treatment of bypassing or "circumventing" what have become known as technical protection mechanisms. TPMs act like digital locks on content such as software, movies, music, and e-books, that control who can access the material and how the material can be used.

TPMs can require an owner to type in a password or code to watch, read, or listen to material, or can "tether" a device or piece of content to a computer on the Internet that is controlled by a copyright holder. Tethered works have to call home, metaphorically speaking, and check that access is permitted before granting it to a user.[7] (One might recall early iTunes music and current iTunes movies as examples of media with this characteristic. In order to play a rented or purchased movie, the account that purchased it must be signed in to iTunes. When a person signs in, his or her computer "calls home" to Apple, and Apple's computers validate the account's password, permitting the movie to be played.) TPMs can also limit functionality, such as by preventing someone from printing a paper copy of an e-book, or by only allowing someone to access a work for a certain period of time.

Before the DMCA, copying digital works without permission already constituted prima facie copyright infringement, and could be punished by statutory fines of up to $100,000 per infringement.[8] (This amount was increased to $150,000 in 1999.)[9] But content owners, such as record labels and motion picture producers, feared that despite these fines they would lose control of their content as computers became more powerful and the Internet became more popular. Computers and the Internet would make the copying and sharing of movies, music, and software substantially easier.

One strategy to prevent such loss of control, they realized, would be to add TPMs, or digital locks, to content, so that software and digital content could only be used or copied with the copyright holder's permission. These measures not only would prevent illegal copying, but also could be used to prevent all copying, including copying for fair-use purposes, such as copying and pasting a long passage from an e-book for use in a book review or term paper.

But the problem with locking up content is that it can sometimes be unlocked without permission—often fairly easily. Before the DMCA, a person or corporation could legally build a device or write computer code to unlock content and remove any controls that copyright holders had placed on it.

But copyright holders didn't want to risk losing control of digital content, when there was so much more potential to control copyrighted works than there had ever been before. Neither traditional analog technology nor the copyright statute had ever granted copyright holders control over how lawfully made copies could be used. But TPMs and digital rights management technology meant that companies could license limited-time-use movies and e-books, or movies and books that could only be accessed under certain circumstances or on particular machines. Fast-forwarding through commercials could be prohibited. Copies could be controlled long after they were sold: in one notorious case, Amazon actually deleted copies of George Orwell's 1984 from customers' Kindles when it realized the copies had not been properly licensed.[10] Whereas analog technology simply didn't allow a publisher to control how many times you read a book or how many photocopies of a favorite poem you made, digital technology could do it.

The way for copyright holders to secure control of digital works was to amend the Copyright Act to forbid both the circumvention of TPMs and the development of circumventing technology. This amendment became the first of two key sections of the DMCA. The second key section of the DMCA, which ultimately became section 512 of the Copyright Act, was negotiated in the face of opposition by Internet and online service providers to the DMCA's anticircumvention provisions and to the Clinton administration's white paper on intellectual property rights.[11] Section 512 provides significant immunity to Internet service providers, in light of the white paper's assertion that almost any digital copy constitutes a prima facie violation of the copyright statute.[12] It provides a "safe harbor" for Internet and online service providers who transmit copyrighted material over the Internet, who store copyright-infringing material at the direction of a user, or who link to infringing material. Whereas the white paper's interpretation of the Copyright Act would have rendered every Internet and online service provider directly liable for the copyright-infringing actions of its users, the safe harbor immunizes providers from liability if they comply with certain requirements in the statute.

In order to qualify for the safe harbor, providers that store or link to content must participate in what is known as "notice and takedown," which essentially means that providers must "take down" content after they are notified that it may be copyright-infringing. Section 512 provides a host such as YouTube or a search engine such as Google with immunity from liability for hosting copyright-infringing videos uploaded by a user, or for linking to webpages containing copyright-infringing material. In return, these service providers must remove the material or link if asked by a copyright holder. In the case of a service provider, such as YouTube, that stores material at the direction of users, the provider must notify the user that material has been taken down, and the user has the option to give "counter-notice" that the material is not infringing, in which case the material can be restored 10 days after the counter-notice is received.[13] There is no obligation for a search engine to notify parties that their material has been removed from its search index, nor are there counter-notification procedures written into the law that provide a process for restoring such links.[14]

With the addition of section 512, President Clinton signed the DMCA into law on October 28, 1998. The final version of the anti-circumvention amendments contained two provisions.

First, in what became section 1201(a) of the Copyright Act, the law prohibited people from "circumventing" a TPM that controlled access to a copyrighted work—or, in other words, from breaking digital locks without permission.[15] There was no exception for circumventing a work for traditional fair uses, such as comment, criticism, or parody, or to access a public-domain work that was controlled alongside a copyrighted work. Rather, the statute allowed the Librarian of Congress to carve out exceptions to the circumvention prohibition via a triennial rulemaking procedure.[16]

Second, in what became section 1201(b), the creation of tools (usually software) to facilitate circumvention was also forbidden, even if the tools were necessary to make certain fair uses of the copyrighted material.[17] Neither the Librarian of Congress nor any other regulatory body has the power to issue exceptions to the 1201(b) prohibition. Thus, while the librarian can announce an exception that would allow individuals to circumvent a TPM, it remains perversely illegal for any third party to create a tool to allow them do so.[18] For example, the exceptions currently allow a visually impaired person to enable a computer to read a protected e-book out loud. But unlocking an e-book's read-aloud function requires someone to write software to gain access to the e-book. Most people don't have the skills to do this and would have to rely on programs written by others. But under 1201(b), it is illegal for a third-party programmer to write a computer program to access the read-aloud function of a locked-up e-book, even though a visually impaired person could legally use that software if he or she acquired it.

Remedies for civil violations of the anticircumvention provisions are up to $2,500 of statutory damages per act of infringement, or the "actual" damages incurred (in other words, the actual amount of financial damage suffered due to the circumvention).[19] But the injunctive and criminal remedies are where the DMCA really has bite. Courts are empowered to enjoin the use, dissemination, or creation of anticircumvention devices to prevent or restrain circumvention,[20] and upon finding a violation of the anticircumvention provisions, to order "the destruction of any device or product involved in the violation that is in the custody or control of the violator."[21] Repeated violations of section 1201 can result in triple damages.[22]

The criminal penalties for violating section 1201 are much more significant. "Any person who violates section 1201 . . . willfully and for purposes of commercial advantage or private financial gain . . . shall be fined not more than $500,000 or imprisoned for not more than 5 years, or both, for the first offense."[23] The punishment can be doubled for subsequent offenses.[24]

EFFECTS ON COMPETITION AND FAIR USE

Section 1201 not only makes certain technologies illegal, but also reduces competition among technology makers. How this works is best illustrated by comparing how technology interacted with copyrighted material before and after the DMCA. When the VHS cassette tape was introduced, any company could legally produce a VCR that could play the tape on a television set. VHS tapes were not burdened with technical protection mechanisms; when moviemakers started selling films on VHS tapes, their content was not scrambled or locked up. As a result, many different companies could produce VCRs and compete with one another to make the best product.

In contrast, DVDs are encoded with a technical protection mechanism called the Content Scrambling System, or CSS. In order to play a DVD, a device needs to decode the scrambled contents of the DVD. CSS was cracked in 1999, and the decryption program, called DeCSS, was made available on the Internet.[25] DeCSS was beneficial not only to those who wanted to copy DVDs illegally, but also to anyone who wanted to copy portions of DVDs for fair uses—people such as film professors and students. But due to section 1201, an aspiring producer of DVD players could not simply incorporate DeCSS into a player without violating the law. DVD players can only legally descramble CSS with permission from the industry group that licenses the CSS standard, the DVD Copy Control Association (DVD CCA).[26] And the Copy Control Association will only license DVD players if the players' manufacturer agrees to respect competition-restricting regional codes and restrictions on fast-forwarding through opening ads.[27] In addition to acting as a gatekeeper for DVD player manufacturers, the DVD CCA also discourages computer users from switching to alternative operating systems. For example, no licensed DVD playing software is currently available for the Linux operating system, although PC and Apple users can easily play their DVDs legally.[28] This means that Linux users who purchase a DVD at a Target store cannot legally play it on their computers.

The situation with DVDs is representative of the effects of the DMCA on many software and content platforms. Because the DVD CCA must give permission before companies can create DVD players, it has the power to dramatically affect the market for DVDs and DVD players, keeping new entrants out of the market or putting them at a significant disadvantage by disallowing certain functionalities in their DVD players. This is a significant departure from the past. Film producers and distributors could not prevent VCRs from having a fast-forward button, but they can control digital content players' functionality by only licensing machines that comply with certain conditions.

Worse effects arise from the absence of a fair use provision in section 1201. The Librarian of Congress can grant exceptions to the circumvention provisions for parties engaged in particular activities, but these exceptions are much narrower than the fair use exceptions to copyright. In 2010, the librarian only approved six exceptions, including enabling an e-book's read-aloud function, enabling interoperability of lawfully obtained software applications on a phone, and circumventing CSS for educational purposes, documentary filmmaking, and noncommercial videos.[29] But even when exceptions are granted to people who have legitimate, legal reasons to circumvent TPMs, the DMCA includes a Kafkaesque twist. The Librarian of Congress cannot grant exceptions for people who create tools to circumvent TPMs. So anyone who creates a way for the visually impaired to listen to encrypted e-books, or for a documentary filmmaker to decrypt a DVD, risks not only fines but up to five years of prison time. Moreover, the permitted exceptions have become much less useful for ordinary people. Those without the technical skills to circumvent a protection measure themselves must either give up or try to acquire an illegally created tool in order to legally access or copy material.

As a result of the DMCA, the development of technologies to help people legally access locked-up material is strongly discouraged. Well-meaning developers from other countries have even avoided coming to the United States for fear of being jailed for the creation of TPM-cracking technologies.[30] Their concern is not unjustified. In 2001, Russian programmer Dmitry Sklyarov was imprisoned for several weeks, and then detained in the United States for several months, after speaking at a conference in Las Vegas. Sklyarov worked for a Russian company, ElcomSoft, and had allegedly worked on a program that converted Adobe e-books into PDF files, removing usage restrictions in the process.[31] The converted e-books could then be read aloud to the visually impaired with text-to-speech software, printed on paper, or read on an unsupported operating system like Linux.[32] While Sklyarov was ultimately allowed to return to Russia,[33] his arrest has exerted a chilling effect on well-meaning American and foreign programmers alike.

In effect, the DMCA has created a new, shadow copyright regime that gives copyright holders the legal power to dramatically curtail fair use. If you want to make a fair-use copy of a digital work, which would be completely legal if made from a VHS tape or a book, you could be liable under the DMCA for circumventing a TPM, or creating a mechanism to circumvent the TPM.

The only way to make fair-use copies of copyrighted works controlled with a TPM is, ironically, to take advantage of the illegal acts and piracy of others. Imagine you wanted to copy a few seconds of protected songs for use in an educational presentation comparing different pieces of music. This would be a fair use of the copyrighted songs, because the copying and performance of the songs would be used for the purpose of commenting on the music.[34] But if the songs were protected, you would be unable to copy the sound clips. However, if someone else developed a program to access the songs and then placed an unprotected version of the song on a file-sharing website, you might be able to copy the songs legally in order to make the fair-use clips. But this copying would require the willingness to navigate often-suspicious sites that traffic in copyright-infringing material. As a result, the DMCA incentivizes honest users to acquiesce to greater control over their own lawfully acquired media.

SITUATING THE DMCA IN HISTORY

Given the historical origins of copyright, it is ironic that a statute rendering specific technologies illegal has become part of the law. The first copyright statute was established in England and was born out of criticism of the printing acts, which had restricted the number of printing presses and required presses to be licensed by the government.[35] The Printing Act of 1662 explicitly limited the number of master printers in England to 20 and the number of presses each master printer could own to two.[36] Calls for "liberty of the press" grew as the 17th century went on. John Milton advocated getting rid of the licensing requirements for printers, so that truth could "be sorted out in debate."[37] Both John Locke and Daniel Defoe argued for a system of authors' rights in their works, rather than for continued regulation of the presses.[38]

The last Printing Act lapsed in 1695, and the Stationers Guild, the members of which had held a monopoly on printing, argued for regulation of the printing presses to be restored, citing the evils of literary piracy as justification for tighter control.[39] These efforts ultimately failed.

In 1710, Parliament enacted the first recognizable copyright act, granting authors an exclusive right to publish their works for 14 years, renewable for another 14.[40] Known as the Statute of Anne, England's first copyright law was effectively a less-restrictive alternative to the rules that had previously restrained the printing industry.

The birth of copyright law paved the way for freedom of the press.[41] Now that printers no longer needed licenses, any individual had the "liberty to print what he would speak."[42] Although stationers lamented the end of printing licensing, claiming it would open the door for increased literary piracy, other values, which were later labeled freedom of speech and of the press, came to trump concerns about piracy—and rightly so.

The relationship between copyright and freedom of the press was also apparent during the founding era of the United States. Before the addition of the Bill of Rights to the Constitution, Antifederalists worried that the copyright clause in the constitution would give Congress the power to curtail freedom of the press, just as England had once used the printing acts to control literary piracy and suppress dissenting views.[43] Federalist James Iredell argued that an amendment protecting freedom of the press was unnecessary, because "Congress will have no other authority over [liberty of the press] than to secure to authors for a limited time an exclusive privilege of publishing their works."[44]

A growing number of scholars, including Eugene Volokh, have argued that the First Amendment's free press clause protects "freedom of the press-as-technology" as opposed to the "press-as-industry" (i.e., journalists).[45] Volokh specifically argues that the free press clause protects everyone's use of the printing press "and its modern equivalents."[46] Indeed, in 1948, the Supreme Court noted, "We have no doubt that moving pictures, like newspapers and radio, are included in the press whose freedom is guaranteed by the First Amendment."[47] Chief Justice Warren E. Burger similarly stated in his concurrence in *First National Bank of Boston v. Bellotti*, "It is not strange that 'press,' the word for what was then the sole means of broad dissemination of ideas and news, would be used to describe the freedom to communicate with a large, unseen audience."[48]

The DMCA is a 300-year step backward for copyright law and freedom of the press.[49] The tremendous insight of the Statute of Anne was that it granted freedom to utilize the *technology* used for copying, while still granting individuals monopoly on the publication of particular works. As a result, printed speech could flourish, and better printers could be developed through market processes. The importance of this change was later enshrined in the US Constitution's First Amendment, which forbids the federal government from making any law abridging freedom of the press.

The DMCA reverses this trend. The anticircumvention provisions criminalize technology that can be used to legally and legitimately access and disseminate speech. Worse, the anticircumvention provisions are ultimately ineffective at preventing piracy—after all, in most cases, it only takes one circumventor to crack a TPM and place a file online. Yet the DMCA prevents the existence of free, competitive, legal markets in content-accessing hardware and software.

"NOTICE AND TAKEDOWN" CURBS FREE EXPRESSION

Unfortunately, section 512's notice-and-takedown system also fails to sufficiently protect free expression and has been routinely abused by copyright holders and other parties. Because takedowns are automatic, the notice-and-takedown process can be actively, intentionally abused in order to censor speech. The Romney campaign ad provides an excellent example: although it's not clear why the Romney takedown notice was issued, it's difficult to imagine that whoever issued it at BMG was motivated by concerns about copyright infringement—especially when videos of Obama singing "Let's Stay Together" had been on YouTube for months and initially remained up. (BMG later issued takedown notices for those videos, presumably because it looked bad to have only targeted Romney's use of the clip and no one else's.)[50]

Other examples of notice-and-takedown abuse abound. Consider one from late 2011, when the public was actively debating the wisdom of the proposed Stop Online Piracy Act. Blogger Michael Masnick wrote a blog post about why SOPA should not be passed, and later discovered that it had been "taken down" from Google's search results.[51] The takedown request was issued by the antipiracy firm Armovore on behalf of a pornography company, Paper Street Cash. (Notably, Google did not have to inform Masnick that his page was being excluded from search results.)[52] There was nothing even arguably infringing, nor any reference to Paper Street Cash or its copyrighted material, in the post or comments, and Google eventually reinstated the blog post in its search index. After Masnick wrote about the takedown, Armovore reached out to "'accept full responsibility for the mistake' and insist that while that takedown was an automated keyword-based effort, they now only do manual takedowns."[53] Masnick accepted Armovore's explanation that the takedown was an honest mistake, as opposed to an attempt to silence opposition to SOPA. Nonetheless, the process would have played out the same way regardless of whether Armovore had acted negligently or maliciously.

Other examples of abuse abound. One group had all Justin Bieber's songs temporarily removed from YouTube as a prank.[54] One Internet celebrity reportedly started using notice-and-takedown to censor videos criticizing him, despite not even having a colorable copyright claim against his critics.[55] Google received a notice from Sony to take down a blog post by romance author Adele Dubois for unclear reasons, possibly because Sony confused her blog posts with copyrighted material concerning the singer Adele.[56]

Even a clip from the NASA control room after the landing of the Mars *Curiosity* rover was briefly removed due to a completely unjustified takedown request.[57]

To further exacerbate the censoring effects of notice-and-takedown, content holders are increasingly automating their notice process. Warner Bros., for example, has been using an automatic process to send takedown notices that yields a significant number of false positives, resulting in significant amounts of non-infringing material being taken down without just cause.[58] (The Electronic Frontier Foundation is currently arguing that such automated takedowns should subject Warner Bros. to liability for misrepresenting infringement to service providers.)[59]

In short, the notice-and-takedown regime requires modern-day presses—online service providers—to censor speakers.[60] Although the government is not directly licensing or censoring speakers, the notice-and-takedown provision forces service providers to do the censoring for others, at the risk of significant legal penalties. As was demonstrated when Michael Masnick's criticism of SOPA was eliminated from Google searches and when Romney's campaign ad was removed from YouTube, the potential for someone to use the law to censor rather than to protect copyrights is enormous.

CONCLUSION

Despite the intertwined history of copyright law and liberty of the press, the relationship between copyright and the First Amendment has gotten short shrift by the Supreme Court. In *Eldred v. Ashcroft*, the Supreme Court justices explained they would not apply traditional First Amendment reasoning to copyright law, arguing that because the First Amendment and the Copyright Clause of the Constitution were passed close in time, it was plain that the founders considered the provisions to be consistent with each other.[61] So long as the "traditional contours" of copyright law were not altered, copyright laws would be upheld as not violative of the First Amendment.[62] The Court specified the traditional

"First Amendment accommodations" that were already "built in" to copyright law: the fair use defense and the "idea / expression distinction" (i.e., the notion that you can copyright particular *expressions* but not *ideas*).[63]

The reasoning of a later case, *Golan v. Holder*, suggests that the "traditional contours" language will not go far to protect the public from expansive, speech-restricting copyright laws.[64] And the Second Circuit Court of Appeals was even willing to uphold an injunction against a website for publishing the DeCSS code.[65] But even in light of these decisions, there is a strong case to be made that the DMCA alters the traditional contours of copyright law, by rendering illegal certain speech-facilitating technology, and by dramatically curtailing the reach of fair use in digital content protected by technical measures. After all, *Eldred* specifically named fair use as a traditional, speech-protecting aspect of copyright law.

The DMCA—including both the anticircumvention provisions and the safe harbors—is not sufficiently protective of First Amendment values. But whether the law is technically unconstitutional is almost beside the point. As the English implicitly acknowledged when the printing acts lapsed, there are competing values at stake when regulating media. There's the goal of providing incentives to publish, but there are also the goals of free expression, competition, and innovation. The DMCA, as well as any future changes proposed to the Copyright Act, must be understood in terms of these goals. And because the DMCA is so woefully unprotective of speech and restrictive to competition, it must be reconsidered.

NOTES

1. See "Political Payoffs and Middle Class Layoffs," YouTube video, 0:36, posted by "mittromney," July 16, 2012, http://www.youtube.com /watch?v=GIajeW6xPnI; Timothy B. Lee, "Music Publisher Uses DMCA to Take Down Romney Ad of Obama Crooning," *Ars Technica* (blog), July 16, 2012, http://arstechnica.com/tech-policy/2012/07

/major-label-uses-dmca-to-take-down-romney-ad-of-obama
-crooning/.

2. See Wendy Seltzer, "Free Speech Unmoored in Copyright's Safe Harbor: Chilling Effects of the DMCA on the First Amendment," *Harvard
   Journal of Law & Technology* 24 (2010): 171–73.

3. Lee, "Music Publisher Uses DMCA to Take Down Romney Ad."

4. Seltzer, "Free Speech Unmoored," 172.

5. See 17 U.S.C. § 107: "The fair use of a copyrighted work, including such
   use by reproduction in copies or phonorecords or by any other means
   specified by that section, for purposes such as criticism, comment,
   news reporting, teaching (including multiple copies for classroom
   use), scholarship, or research, is not an infringement of copyright."

6. See 17 U.S.C. § 1201–5 (anticircumvention provisions); 17 U.S.C. § 512
   (safe harbor provision).

7. Jonathan Zittrain, "The Future of the Internet and How to Stop It" (New
   Haven and London: Yale University Press, 2008), 104–5.

8. Congress doubled the range of statutory damages in 1989, to a maximum of $100,000 per willful infringement. *Berne Convention Imple-
   mentation Act of 1988*, Public Law 100–568, 102 Stat. 2853 (1988);
   Pamela Samuelson and Tara Wheatland, "Statutory Damages in Copyright Law: A Remedy in Need of Reform," *William and Mary Law Review*
   51 (2009): 439, 455n62.

9. See *Digital Theft Deterrence and Copyright Damages Improvement Act of
   1999*, Public Law 106–160, 113 Stat. 1774 (1999).

10. Brad Stone, "Amazon Erases Orwell Books from Kindle," *New York Times*,
    July 18, 2009, http://www.nytimes.com/2009/07/18/technology
    /companies/18amazon.html.

11. Jessica Litman, *Digital Copyright* (New York: Prometheus Books, 2006),
    134–35.

12. Ibid., 94–95: cites Information Infrastructure Task Force, *Intellectual
    Property and the National Information Infrastructure: The Report of the
    Working Group on Intellectual Property Rights* (Amherst, New York: Pro-
    metheus Books, 1995), http://www.uspto.gov/web/offices/com/doc
    /ipnii/, 19–130.

13. 17 U.S.C. § 512(g).

14. See 17 U.S.C. § 512(g) (specifying restoration and counter-notification procedures for material stored with a service provider, but not for material discoverable through information-location tools).

15. 17 U.S.C. § 1201(a)(1)(A).

16. 17 U.S.C. § 1201(a)(1)(C)–(D).

17. The statute stated, "No person shall manufacture, import, offer to the public, provide, or otherwise traffic" in any technology or service that is "primarily designed or produced for the purpose of circumventing a [TPM]; . . . has only limited commercially significant purpose or use other than to circumvent a [TPM]; or . . . is marketed . . . with that person's knowledge for use in circumventing a [TPM]." 17 U.S.C. § 1201(a) (2), (b).

18. Some other, very limited exceptions to the anticircumvention provisions were included in the statute for nonprofit libraries, archives, educational institutions, law enforcement, intelligence, other government activities, reverse engineering, encryption research, and security testing. See 17 U.S.C. § 1201(d)–(j).

19. 17 U.S.C. § 1203(c).

20. 17 U.S.C. § 1203(b)(1).

21. 17 U.S.C. § 1203(b)(6).

22. 17 U.S.C. § 1203(c)(4).

23. 17 U.S.C. § 1204(a)(1).

24. 17 U.S.C. § 1204(a)(2).

25. Universal City Studios v. Corley, 273 F.3d 429, 437 (2d. Cir. 2001).

26. See DVD Copy Control Association website, accessed July 15, 2012, http://www.dvdcca.org/.

27. Timothy B. Lee, "Circumventing Competition: The Perverse Consequences of the Digital Millennium Copyright Act" (Cato Institute Policy Analysis No. 564, March 21, 2006), http://www.cato.org/pubs /pas/pa564.pdf.

28. Wendy Seltzer, "The Imperfect Is the Enemy of the Good," *Berkeley Technology Law Journal* 25 (2011): 909, 947n171.

29. 37 C.F.R. § 201.40 (2010).

30. See Fred Von Lohmann, *Unintended Consequences: Twelve Years under the DMCA* (Electronic Frontier Foundation, Feb. 2010), 6.

31. Ibid., 5–6.

32. Ibid., 11.

33. Ibid., 6.

34. See 17 U.S.C. § 107 ("[T]he fair use of a copyrighted work . . . for purposes such as criticism, comment, news reporting, teaching . . . , scholarship, or research, is not an infringement of copyright.").

35. Edward Lee, "Freedom of the Press 2.0," *Georgia Law Review* 42 (2008): 309, 322–23.

36. Ibid., 323.

37. Ibid., 324; see also Lyman Ray Patterson, *Copyright in Historical Perspective* (Nashville, Vanderbilt University Press, 1968), 114.

38. Lee, "Freedom of the Press," 325.

39. Ibid.

40. 8 Anne, ch. 19. The statute also granted a copyright for 21 years to books already in print and preserved the "printing patent," a right to publish a work that was granted by the sovereign. Ibid.; Patterson, *Copyright in Historical Perspective*, 78–80, 143.

41. "Copyright was born with freedom of the press, not against it." Lee, "Freedom of the Press," 330.

42. John Locke, *Locke: Political Essays*, ed. Mark Goldie (Cambridge University Press, 1997), 331.

43. Lee, "Freedom of the Press," 334.

44. James Iredell, *Answers to Mr. Mason's Objections to the New Constitution* (1788), reprinted in *Pamphlets on the Constitution of the United States 1787–1788*, ed. Paul L. Ford (1888), http://files.libertyfund.org/files/1670/Ford_1338.pdf, 360–61.

45. See, e.g., Eugene Volokh, "Freedom for the Press as an Industry, or for the Press as a Technology? From the Framing to Today," *University of Pennsylvania Law Review* 160 (2012): 459; Lee, "Freedom of the Press," 339–56; David A. Anderson, "Freedom of the Press," *Texas Law Review* 80 (2002): 429, 446–47: "To the generation of the Framers of the First Amendment, 'the press' meant 'the printing press.' It referred less to a journalistic enterprise than to the technology of printing and the opportunities for communication that the technology created. 'Freedom of the press' referred to the freedom of the people to publish their

views, rather than the freedom of journalists to pursue their craft."

46. Volokh, "Freedom for the Press as an Industry, or for the Press as a Technology?," 462.

47. United States v. Paramount Pictures, 334 U.S. 131, 166 (1948).

48. 435 U.S. 765, 800n5 (Chief Justice Burger, concurring).

49. The first "step backward" was actually the Audio Home Recording Act, passed in 1992, which required producers of digital audio recording devices to incorporate a copy protection system into their products and forbade circumvention of the system. 17 U.S.C. § 1002(a), (c). However, the act became comparatively insignificant when digital audio recording devices failed to gain popularity.

50. Mike Masnick, "Even Obama Is a Pirate: BMG Issues New Takedown on Original Obama Singing Al Green Clip," Techdirt (blog), July 17, 2012, http://www.techdirt.com/articles/20120717/13500819733/bmg -doubles-down-issues-takedown-original-clip-obama-singing-al -green.shtml.

51. Mike Masnick, "Key Techdirt SOPA/PIPA Post Censored by Bogus DMCA Takedown Notice," Techdirt (blog), Feb. 27, 2012, http://www .techdirt.com/articles/20120223/15102217856/key-techdirt-sopapipa -post-censored-bogus-dmca-takedown-notice.shtml.

52. See notes 14–15 and accompanying text.

53. Mike Masnick, "Company That Issued Bogus Takedown Says It Was All a Mistake, Apologizes," Techdirt (blog), Feb. 28, 2012, http://www .techdirt.com/articles/20120228/09424117897/company-that-issued -bogus-takedown-says-it-was-all-mistake-apologizes.shtml.

54. "Justin Bieber Music Videos Yanked from YouTube," TMZ, Aug 29, 2011, http://www.tmz.com/2011/08/29/justin-bieber-music-video -vevo-youtube-hacked-ilcreation-baby-somebody-to-love-that -should-be-me.

55. Mike Masnick, "Double Bogus DMCA Takedown All The Way!," Techdirt (blog), Sept. 7, 2011, http://www.techdirt.com/articles /20110907/09453415839/double-bogus-dmca-takedown-all-way .shtml.

56. Mike Masnick, "Romance Author Adele Dubois Receives Take- down on Blog Post for Having the Same Name as Singer Adele,"

Techdirt (blog), May 18, 2012, http://www.techdirt.com/articles
/20120517/17443418961/romance-author-adele-dubois-receives
-takedown-blog-post-having-same-name-as-singer-adele.shtml.

57. Eric Limer, "NASA's Official Mars Landing Video Got Taken off You-
Tube over Bogus Copyright Claims," *Gizmodo* (blog), Aug. 6, 2012,
http://gizmodo.com/5932089/nasas-official-rover-landing-video
-got-taken-off-youtube-over-bogus-copyright-claims.

58. Dragos Pirvu, "Automated DMCA Takedown Notices Are Illegal
and They Must Be Sanctioned, Says EFF," *Unbiased Tech*, March
9, 2012, http://www.unbiasedtech.com/illegal-automated-dmca
-takedown-notices-eff/; Mike Masnick, "EFF Argues That Automated Bogus DMCA Takedowns Violate the Law and Are Subject to
Sanctions," *Techdirt* (blog), March 8, 2012, http://www.techdirt.com
/articles/20120308/03505018034/eff-argues-that-automated-bogus
-dmca-takedowns-violate-law-are-subject-to-sanctions.shtml.

59. See "EFF Calls Foul on Robo-Takedowns" (Electronic Frontier Foundation, March 6, 2012), https://www.eff.org/press/releases/eff-calls
-foul-robo-takedowns/; 17 U.S.C. § 512(f).

60. See Felix T. Wu, "Collateral Censorship and the Limits of Intermedi-
ary Immunity," *Notre Dame Law Review* 87 (2011): 293–94, 300–4; J. M.
Balkin, "Free Speech and Hostile Environments," *Columbia Law Re-
view* 99 (1999): 2295, 2298–99 (1999); Michael I. Meyerson, "Authors,
Editors, and Uncommon Carriers: Identifying the 'Speaker' within the
New Media," *Notre Dame Law Review* 79 (1995): 116–24.

61. Eldred v. Ashcroft, 537 U.S. 186, 219 (2003).

62. Ibid., 221.

63. Ibid., 219–20.

64. 132 S.Ct. 873 (2012) (rejecting an argument that removing existing
works from the public domain and placing them under copyright violated the traditional contours of copyright law).

65. Universal City Studios, Inc. v. Corley, 273 F.3d 429 (2d. Cir. 2001).

6

The *Times*, They Are A-Changin':
The New Economics of Weak
Copyright Enforcement

Eli Dourado

I N MARCH 2011, the New York Times debuted its new online pay-wall to rumors that its development had cost the company as much as $40 million.[1] Arthur Sulzberger, the *Times'* publisher, insisted that it cost much less, and *paidContent* reported that the real number was close to $25 million.[2] However much the paywall cost, many were aghast at how the *Times* could spend so much on a paywall that barely worked.[3] Before the paywall even officially launched, techies figured out how to disable it. They did so with three lines of JavaScript:

```
$('overlay').hide();
$('gatewayCreative').hide();
$(document.body).setStyle( { overflow:'scroll'
   } );
```

Others did it by injecting only two lines of CSS:

```
#overlay, #gatewayCreative { display:
   none !important; visibility:
   hidden !important;}
body { overflow: scroll !important;  }
```

Even if one does not understand JavaScript or CSS very well, a passing glance at this code shows why it was so easy to get around the paywall. The *Times* implements the paywall so that the requested article is there all along. There are two sections of the page, called "overlay" and "gatewayCreative," that obstruct the user's view of the article. The "body" of the page is instructed to hide any content that does not fit "above the fold," so that the user cannot simply scroll down and read the article. Simply instructing the browser to hide "overlay" and "gatewayCreative" and to allow scrolling on the page's body enables the reader to get to the requested content. What's more, with modern browsers, these instructions can be executed automatically any time a user is browsing nytimes.com. The end result is that anyone with very modest technical skill can configure his web browser to seamlessly bypass the *Times'* paywall. While the code used to implement the paywall has changed a little in the last year, it's still terribly easy to bypass.

How could the *Times* be so incompetent? Is creating a paywall so very difficult? To make matters more curious, consider that the *Times* has had a completely functional and effective paywall (for example) for its crossword puzzles that long predated the main site's paywall. The crossword puzzle paywall operates on a server-side basis and is not easily bypassed. Why would the *Times* implement a faulty news paywall on a client-side basis?

It seems clear that the *Times'* paywall was built to allow circumvention by those determined to circumvent it. The official exceptions to the paywall policy underscore this point. The *Times* originally announced that non-subscribing users would get 20 free articles per month, although this number has now been decreased to 10. In addition, the *Times* participates in Google's "First Click Free" program. This means that users coming from Google search can access articles for free, up to five times per day. Furthermore, users coming from social media sites, such as Facebook, Twitter, and blogs, will not ever hit the paywall, even if they are over their monthly limit. It's understandable why the *Times* would want to allow these exceptions. It offers free articles every month so that potential customers can try out the paper. It accommodates users coming from Google search because these readers would not otherwise have come to the site, so they do not represent lost business. And it does not exclude readers coming from blogs and social networks because it wants its stories to be circulated; people blogging and tweeting its articles is part of what makes the *Times* the newspaper of record, which increases demand for the *Times*.

All these official loopholes can be used to access a particular article without a subscription. For example, if you want to read an article and get stymied by the paywall, search Google or Twitter for the headline and you will breeze right on through to the content. But as the writers of the code above discovered in March 2011, the porous paywall goes further: it allows users who really want to do so to disable all access restrictions semi-permanently. The paywall is not *really* a mechanism for enforcing copyright. Rather, it is a mechanism for sorting and price discrimination.

PRICE DISCRIMINATION IN THE CONTENT BUSINESS

Copyright is a monopoly, and the basic account of monopoly entails some economic inefficiency—what economists call deadweight loss. Suppose I am a widget monopolist, and after the fixed costs of getting my business running, designing the widget, and setting up my factory, it costs me $5 to produce each additional widget. The marginal cost of a widget is $5. If I am to cover my fixed costs and earn a profit, I *must* charge more than $5 per widget. If I charge less than $5 per widget, I would lose money on every widget. If I charge exactly $5 for a widget, then I am not making any profit on that widget, but I am also not covering my fixed costs, and I will go out of business. And, crucially, I maximize my profits not by just charging enough to cover my fixed costs, but by charging more, even if that means I sell fewer widgets.

Suppose that I maximize my profits by selling widgets at $8 each. Some consumers might be unwilling to buy at that price—but they may be willing to pay $6. This is a problem. Economic efficiency demands that every consumer willing to pay the marginal cost of a good consume it. The marginal cost of the widget is only $5, and the customer is willing to pay $6, which means that there are gains from trade—but the trade doesn't happen. This means that we forgo $1 worth of gains between us, the difference between $6 and $5, and that is inefficient. Add up all the losses from all the customers willing to pay more than $5 but less than $8 per widget and you have the total deadweight loss of monopoly.

The deadweight loss is also potentially a forgone profit opportunity. What if I could charge $8 to everyone willing to pay at least that much, but *also* charge a lower price, still above $5, to everyone else? I would make the same amount of profit as before from the customers willing to pay $8, but I would also make some additional profit from the other customers. And consumers as a whole would be better off—those who are willing to pay $8 or more would be no worse off, but at least some other customers would now benefit from widgets they otherwise would not have consumed. Engaging in this *price discrimination* makes total welfare—the sum of the benefits minus costs to everyone—increase.[4]

Creative content is just like a widget, only with a much lower marginal cost. Once a news story has been written, the cost of reproducing it in the Internet age is so low as to be negligible. Call it zero. This means that there are forgone gains from trade if *any* consumer who values the content *at all* is excluded from consuming it. Charging any price above zero to everyone means that there are some profits still left on the table. If the content creator can sort consumers into different groups based on willingness to pay and charge each group an appropriate price, it can earn higher profits and usually improve economic efficiency at the same time.

This is what the *Times'* porous paywall accomplishes: It induces some customers—those who derive enough value from the articles, enjoy affiliating with the *Times*, or don't want to be bothered to circumvent the paywall—to pay what the *Times* defines as "full price." Meanwhile, no other users really get excluded. Everyone else can read the articles they find through search or social networks, and if they really want to read everything, they can. Meanwhile, these users still get served ads, so the *Times* still makes money from their visits, and they are of course more likely to link to the *Times* in their own blog posts and tweets.

A SURPRISING SUCCESS

More than a year after its launch, to the surprise of many observers, the *Times'* paywall appears to be a great success. Back when the paywall launched, Reuters blogger Felix Salmon wrote:

> What does all this mean for the New York Times Company? I can't see how it's good. The paywall is certainly being set high enough that a lot of regular readers will *not* subscribe. These are readers who would normally link to the NYT from their blogs, who would tweet NYT articles, who would post those articles on Facebook, and so on. As a result, not only will traffic from these readers decline, but so will all their referral traffic, too. The NYT makes more than $300 million a year in digital ad revenue, so even a modest decline in pageviews, relative to what the site could have generated sans paywall, can mean many millions of dollars foregone. On top of that, the paywall itself cost somewhere over $40 million to develop.
>
> Against all that, how much revenue will the paywall bring in? A very large number of the paper's most loyal readers are already print subscribers, and get access to the website at no extra cost. So the new revenues from the paywall will only come from people who read the website a lot but who don't subscribe in print.[5]

One year later, the *Times* reported 454,000 paid digital-only subscribers, and most recently, in July 2012, the company reported 509,000 of them.[6] Subscribers pay $15 to $20 every four weeks, depending on whether they get tablet access, so at an average of, say, $17 per subscriber for 13 four-week billing periods per year, that is a rate of over $112 million of revenue per year from subscriptions.

And what about the loss of advertising revenue? In the first fiscal quarter of 2011, before the paywall was introduced, the company's News Media Group, which includes nytimes.com, posted digital advertising revenues of $53.9 million.[7] In the second quarter of 2012, the most recent period for which data are available, digital advertising revenues in the News Media Group were $52.6 million.[8] Annualized, this represents a decline of around $5 million in digital advertising revenues against the estimated $112 million in additional subscription revenues.

As early as July 2011, Salmon had to admit that "the NYT paywall is working."[9] This is not to say that the New York Times Company is now free of financial challenges; the newspaper industry faces more competition than ever from blogs and social media, and there is of course the recession. But all things considered, the *Times'* porous paywall gambit has paid off.

TWO CONTENT FALLACIES

Why was the *Times'* success such a surprise? When people evaluate content and copyright issues, it is common for them to implicitly or explicitly rely on one of two extreme viewpoints. The first extreme view, held most prominently by the record labels, is to approach the content business like business in the world of atoms—to ignore the unique properties of informational goods. There is an assumption that you can't make money by giving your product away, and that property must be defended. Consequently, those who hold this view see people who appropriate content without paying as on a level with criminals. The opposing extreme view, popular among the digerati, is embodied in Stewart Brand's iconic phrase, "Information wants to be free." According to this view, any sort of paywall or access restriction to content is doomed to failure because of the unique properties of the world of bits.

At root, the first view regards enforcement as something that is or should be accounted for as free. But to the contrary, copyright enforcement is costly. Indeed, the cost of deterring or preventing an infringement has skyrocketed in recent decades. For example, an online newspaper could adopt a strict paywall with ease, but it would be costly for it to police the Internet to ensure that bloggers do not quote its articles at length. Even if news sites were to engage in this kind of enforcement—and the record labels do something similar in their policing of YouTube—it would be virtually impossible to prevent legitimate readers from emailing copies of articles to their non-subscribing friends. As the cost of enforcement rises, it is socially efficient to aim to deter fewer instances of infringement. Indeed, in many cases it is also privately rational to do the same, at least if the offended party is the one paying the cost of enforcement. An extreme version of this argument is easy to follow: if it ever became literally impossible to deter any instances of copyright infringement, then it would be foolish to spend resources trying to deter them.

The logic of costly deterrence is amplified by the fact that in the content industry, there are often few benefits to deterring infringement. When you prevent a teenager from illegally downloading your album, you rarely gain a sale of the album; the teenager can always listen to something else. Furthermore, you lose a potential fan who might come to your concert, tell his friends about your music, or buy your T-shirt. The world of bits really is different from the world of atoms. Informational goods are non-rivalrous, so rights enforcement for them is less beneficial than it is for normal, rivalrous goods.

On the other hand, in their exceptionalist zeal for the information economy, a number of technically minded commentators have embraced the opposite extreme. They argue that all forms of access control are doomed. At root, proponents of this view also fail to properly consider the costs and benefits for all populations. It's true that nearly any workable form of access control, whether it be encryption-based digital rights management or a registration-based paywall, is vulnerable to those truly determined to overcome it. But not everyone has such strong determination to get content for free. Many ordinary consumers would rather spend a few bucks than invest the time and energy to circumvent access controls. To them, this time and energy, however small, is a cost of accessing the content, whereas to many playful nerds, it can be a fun challenge to try to find a way around the access control.

There may also be other benefits bundled with the content. A number of users who routinely pirate movies pay to see some of them in the theater; it is hard to match the experience of the big screen. Video game makers can bundle leaderboards and social features with versions of their games that authenticate online. Perhaps the biggest benefit that some users get from paying for content is a good feeling associated with supporting a content producer. The super-rich have patronized artists and thinkers for centuries. Ordinary consumers may share a motivation to contribute to the production of more content, or even just to affiliate with their favorite producers by patronizing them in this small way.

The bottom line is that both of the extreme viewpoints about the nature of the content industry are wrong. A moderate position is more nearly correct. The purpose of access controls should not be to try to exclude all nonpayers, but that does not mean that they have no role. Rather, the role of access controls should increasingly be to induce those users who are willing to pay for access to do so, and to pay no mind to those users who are willing to invest some effort in circumventing them.

WEAK ACCESS CONTROLS ARE THE FUTURE
The *New York Times* may or may not have thought through the paywall in exactly these terms, but nevertheless, the company's strategy is consistent with the analysis above. This example is important because the newspaper industry is in the vanguard with respect to changes wrought by the Internet; news was one of the first popular uses of the web. In particular, news is one of the first content

production domains that the Internet has radically democratized. The up-front costs associated with starting a news website are miniscule compared to those necessary to start a newspaper. This has led to a staggering amount of competition in the market for online news and opinion journalism. While hypercompetition has been bad for incumbent profits, consumers have benefited from greater availability and diversity of content.

Disruption has been slower in other traditional content industries like music and film. But we can be optimistic that disintermediation of these industries is still coming. The tools needed to compete with the record labels have only emerged in the last decade, as distribution platforms for digital music have matured and high-quality audio recording and editing software has dropped in price. Bands are increasingly marketing their own music and tours directly to fans; the decline in the importance of labels is underway. Because of the greater costs associated with producing and marketing movies, the film industry is lagging behind these trends. But what reason is there to doubt that the inexorable march of digital democratization will stop before it disrupts the film industry? As technology improves, it too will become more like the newspaper industry.

If these changes are indeed underway, then it seems reasonable to predict that the slower-changing content industries will ultimately adopt content enforcement strategies that are similar to those used by the industries that have experienced more thoroughgoing change. Some of the details may differ; for example, because news sites can rely more heavily on advertising than other content industries can, they have an incentive to use more porous access control methods. But this is merely a matter of degree. The basic strategy of price discriminating by using access controls to get consumers to self-select into paid and unpriced segments is sound. Consider the hit TV show *Game of Thrones*. Millions of people pirated the show, more than watched it through legitimate channels.[10] Although HBO could have sued infringing users, it did very little to combat this piracy. Instead, HBO basically accepted the piracy because most nonpaying users would not otherwise subscribe to HBO, and because the pirates helped create a stronger buzz for the show, which helped it succeed. Furthermore, the existence of pirated copies of the show did not eliminate the incentive to subscribe, at least for those customers who valued watching the show the day it first aired, in uncompressed high definition, with a minimum of fuss.

As an example of weak copyright enforcement, the case of the *New York Times* paywall also gives some indication of what a world with weaker legal copyright protection would look like. Contrary to what some of the pessimists say, we would still enjoy new content, but content industries that have been slow to adapt would need to change. They might have to explore new business models or embrace creative ways to encourage customers to pay for content. In this important sense, the music and movie industries would have to become more like the news industry.

Of course, this is exactly what a lot of content producers fear. Newspapers have struggled during the transition to the Internet era, and profits have suffered. But the point of copyright is not to protect the profits of content producers; it is to ensure that content production flourishes. On this score, the news industry has never been healthier. We have more options for journalistic content than ever before. There are news sites that are both general and niche, serious and sassy, demure and sensationalist, shortform and longform. One of the biggest problems that Internet users face is coming up with satisfactory *filtering* mechanisms for their online news, there is so much of it. Meanwhile, news sites are finding creative ways to earn enough money to stay in business—in some cases, just barely. And that's just fine.

COPYRIGHT FOR THE 21ST CENTURY

This chapter has argued that weak access controls, like the *New York Times'* porous paywall, represent the future of content monetization. Despite two competing misconceptions about the role of access controls, it is likely that we will see more content producers adopt similar strategies. It is worth asking, therefore, how intellectual property law needs to change to match the reality of how content will be funded and distributed in the 21st century.

First, the law needs to abandon the criminalization of copyright infringement. In a world where content producers are not substantially harmed and possibly even benefit from some level of circumvention of their access controls, it does not make sense to criminalize those who circumvent access controls. Laws like the Digital Millennium Copyright Act make users who disable the *Times'* paywall into criminals. In fact, it is a good thing that the *New York Times* has slightly changed the way its paywall operates in the last year, because otherwise the code at the beginning of this chapter would be illegal to distribute under the DMCA, and those involved in producing and selling this book could face criminal charges. Given that the *Times* spent extra money to make sure that its paywall was especially porous, it seems absurd to criminalize the act of circumventing it. Furthermore, the criminalization of piracy mostly protects those content industries that have been the slowest to adapt to the Internet era. If we want adjustment to happen rapidly, we need to stop subsidizing old business models.

Second, copyright law should focus on commercial infringement only. The *Times* does not enforce its copyright against ordinary "infringing" users, but it derives some benefit from the fact that its competitors cannot engage in wholesale appropriation of its content. The law can differentiate between those who redistribute copyrighted content for profit without permission and those who simply consume it on a noncommercial basis. The benefits of the latter kind of enforcement are low or—as in the case of the *Times'* paywall—negative, and the costs are high. In contrast, enforcement against commercial infringement plausibly has high benefits. It is also less costly to enforce copyrights against commercial infringement, if only because such redistribution is predicated on consumers knowing where to go to get the infringing content.

Most likely, this involves some sort of open and notorious behavior on the part of the infringer, such as advertising or maintaining a home page.

Finally, we need to embrace a stronger role for informal norms than for formal law to ensure that content producers are compensated. A number of people subscribe to the *Times* because it makes them feel good to do so. They may know several of the tricks that people use to penetrate the paywall, but they subscribe anyway. The spirit of patronage is alive and well, but nothing is more likely to destroy it than the feeling that content producers and consumers are on different sides, which is exactly what copyright enforcement engenders. Consequently, we should begin to reevaluate whether formal copyright enforcement is necessary at all. The evidence that it is necessary is surprisingly meager, and there is innovation in several domains, such as joke telling, recipes, sports moves, and fashion, in which copyright does not apply.[11] While customers of the *Times* may not all be conservatives or libertarians, their patronage of content they enjoy is evidence that we don't need the state to promote the progress of science and the useful arts.

NOTES

1. Brett Pulley, "*New York Times* Fixes Paywall Flaws to Balance Free versus Paid on the Web," *Bloomberg.com*, January 28, 2011, http://www.bloomberg.com/news/2011-01-28/new-york-times-fixes-paywall-glitches-to-balance-free-vs-paid-on-the-web.html.

2. Staci D. Kramer, "*New York Times* Paywall Cost: More Like $25 Million," *paidContent*, April 7, 2011, http://paidcontent.org/2011/04/07/419-new-york-times-paywall-cost-more-like-25-million/.

3. Mike Masnick, "It Took the *NY Times* 14 Months and $40 Million Dollars to Build the World's Stupidest Paywall?," *Techdirt* (blog), March 17, 2011, http://www.techdirt.com/articles/20110317/10393913530/it-took-ny-times-14-months-40-million-dollars-to-build-worlds-stupidest-paywall.shtml.

4. This example is not perfectly general. It is *possible* to construct examples where price discrimination reduces total welfare. It is also *easy* to construct examples where total welfare increases, but consumer welfare decreases. In general, where price discrimination causes total output to increase and does not itself impose many costs, price discrimination is almost always welfare-improving.

5. Felix Salmon, "The NYT Paywall Arrives," Reuters (blog), March 17, 2011, http://blogs.reuters.com/felix-salmon/2011/03/17/the-nyt -paywall-arrives/.

6. New York Times Company, "The New York Times Company Reports 2012 First-Quarter Results," press release, April 19, 2012, http://www .nytco.com/pdf/1Q_2012_Earnings.pdf; New York Times Company, "The New York Times Company Reports 2012 Second-Quarter Results," press release, July 26, 2012, http://www.nytco.com/pdf/2Q_2012 _Earnings.pdf. This figure includes digital subscribers to the *International Herald Tribune*, which is owned by the New York Times Company and features some of the same content. The New York Times Company does not break down the numbers further.

7. New York Times Company, "The New York Times Company Reports 2011 First-Quarter Results," press release, April 21, 2011, http://www .nytco.com/pdf/1Q_2011_Earnings.pdf.

8. New York Times Company, "The New York Times Company Reports 2012 Second-Quarter Results."

9. Felix Salmon, "The NYT Paywall Is Working," Reuters (blog), July 26, 2011, http://blogs.reuters.com/felix-salmon/2011/07/26/the-nyt -paywall-is-working/.

10. Casey Chan, "More People Pirate *Game of Thrones* Than Watch *Game of Thrones* on HBO," Gizmodo (blog), June 8, 2012, http://gizmodo .com/5916885/more-people-pirate-game-of-thrones-than-watch -game-of-thrones-on-hbo.

11. Kal Raustiala and Christopher Jon Sprigman, *The Knockoff Economy: How Imitation Sparks Innovation* (New York: Oxford University Press, 2012).

7
Five Reforms for Copyright

Tom W. Bell

O N NOVEMBER 28, 2009, police arrested a 22-year-old Chicago woman named Samantha Tumpach, jailed her for two nights, and charged her with "criminal use of a motion picture exhibition"—a felony offense punishable with up to three years in prison. Her crime? She had captured two brief clips of *The Twilight Saga: New Moon* while recording her family's surprise birthday celebration for her sister, who had come to the theater to watch the film.[1] Tumpach copied under four minutes of the movie in total and obviously had no intention of making a bootleg for resale. "You can hear me talking the whole time," she explained.[2] Officials eventually dropped the charges, but the damage had been done. Tumpach brought suit for malicious prosecution, intentional infliction of emotional distress, negligence, and defamation.[3] Her complaint did not, however, name the ultimate cause of her distress: a copyright regime that has grown too big and too powerful.

How should we reform copyright? By treating it the same way we should treat federal farm subsidies, Medicare, or any one of a number of big government programs. If you doubt whether politicians and bureaucrats can do a good job of regulating agricultural production or health care, you should also doubt the efficacy of the Copyright Act, through which the federal government comprehensively regulates markets in original books, movies, plays, photographs, emails, videos, computer programs, and other expressive works. Copyright represents at best a necessary evil. More likely, it offers us a Faustian bargain of dubious propriety. We can best improve copyright by limiting its power, repairing its foundations, and opening up ways to escape it entirely.

That is not the typical approach to copyright reform, concededly. On one hand, most policy wonks regard copyright as a well-intentioned but clunky government program that they might save with only a bit of tinkering around the edges (though what copyright needs saving from—whether industry lobbyists[4] or rampaging pirates[5]—depends on which analyst you ask). On the other hand, a few philosophically minded commentators decry copyright as an unjustifiable imposition on individual liberties and, as such, deserving immediate abolition.[6] You would not end slavery in steps, would you?[7] So too, these critics ask of copyright.

This chapter offers a third approach to copyright reform, one that pays due respect to copyright's honorable origins and potential benefits but that warily regards it as a growing infringement on individual liberty. The reforms described here constrain copyright within its proper limits while encouraging us to explore, cautiously and incrementally, how far we can go toward a copyright-free world. Below follow the details of five specific reforms:

1. Reinstate the Founders' Copyright Act,
2. Withdraw the US from the Berne Convention,
3. Develop misuse doctrine into an escape from copyright,
4. Focus copyright policy on consumers' costs, not producers' profits, and
5. Reconceive "IP" as "Intellectual *Privilege*."

Before fleshing out these proposed reforms, however, it bears asking whether copyright needs fixing in the first place. It does— but not for the reasons that you might at first expect. The next section explains.

TOWARD FREEDOM

Is copyright in crisis? It has critics, of course, but nobody really knows how bad things have gotten. Despite prominent claims that the copyright law strikes a "delicate balance" between public and private rights, we cannot measure its success or failure with anything like precision. News stories occasionally suggest that copyright law has grown too powerful, as when Samantha Tumpach was arrested for incidentally recording bits of *Twilight*, but that provides merely anecdotal evidence.

Policy wonks demand better, but copyright's breadth, intangibility, and heterogeneity will leave them frustrated. The problem arises not merely from the manifold variables at stake—words published, poems read, lines coded, scenes shot—but from the incommensurable values affected by copyright. We should reform copyright not in pursuit of policy perfection, an impossible dream, but in defense of freedom.

At root, copyright recalls a proverbial deal with the devil. In pursuit of "the Progress of Science and useful Arts," the Constitution empowers Congress to "secur[e] for limited Times to Authors . . . the exclusive Right to their . . . Writings."[8] Lawmakers responded to that invitation by passing the Copyright Act, a federal statute that now comprehensively regulates the production and distribution of books, plays, movies, programs, and other fixed expressive works. Did the public come out ahead under that Faustian bargain? We might ask the same question of federal regulation of agricultural subsidies, health care, home mortgages, or education. Different analysts will answer with different numbers, all of them mere approximations and none of it sufficient to decide the choice between comfortable servitude and daring independence.

Copyright, as a legal regime, is not in crisis; it grows and thrives. The first Copyright Act, passed in 1790 by many of the same people who founded the United States, includes just seven sections and 1,308 words and fills fewer than two pages.[9] Since then the US Copyright Office has taken root in the Library of Congress and grown like a vast canopy of vines over copyright. *Circular 92*, the office's most recent compendium of the laws under its purview, weighs in at more than 350 pages and 150,000 words.[10] Separately from those statutory provisions, the Copyright Office's own detailed and voluminous regulations run (or rather plod) to more than 170 sections and uncounted words.[11] As the graph opposite demonstrates, the term of US copyrights has steadily expanded over the years.[12] Other comparisons between the Founders' law and the present law follow in the next section, which describes the good old days of the 1790 Copyright Act. It all goes to show that we should not fear for copyright; we should fear for our liberties.

The five copyright reforms described below do not come with any guarantee of net social welfare gains. They guarantee only increased freedom. Although that will doubtless suffice for some readers, those more accustomed to cost–benefit analyses should note that copyright, as a scheme for federally regulating markets in expressive works, probably falls far short of optimal efficiency. Lawmakers have already tried massive doses of statism. Their recent innovations include retroactively extending copyright terms, controlling the design of consumer electronics, authorizing ex parte seizures of domain names, and creating a new "IP Czar."[13]

We can surely do better than more of the same. Quantitative certainty will continue to elude us and minor tweaks to the status quo will not suffice. Instead, we need to pursue a new direction in copyright reform: toward freedom.

REVIVE THE FOUNDERS' COPYRIGHT ACT

You find yourself trapped between a lumbering but hungry bear and a deep, narrow chasm. After quickly calculating the downsides of wrestling your way out of trouble, you decide to jump across to safety. You need a running start first, though, so you back up a few steps. Only then do you run to the edge and leap to your freedom. So, too, with copyright reform: To make our way forward, we must first step back.

Trend of Copyright Duration in US Law

Legend:
- Sonny Bono Act ('98)
- 1976 Act
- 1962–74 Acts
- 1909 Act
- 1831 Act
- 1790 Act

DURATION OF BASIC COPYRIGHT TERM (YEARS)

YEAR COPYRIGHT TERM BEGAN

US copyright law begins in the Constitution, ratified in 1789, and the 1790 Copyright Act that followed quickly thereafter.[14] Beyond the words themselves, which empower Congress to "promote the Progress of Science and useful Arts, by securing for limited Times to Authors . . . the exclusive Right to their . . . Writings," we have little evidence about what the Constitution means of copyright.[15] Notes from the Philadelphia Convention hardly mention the topic, nor did copyright get much analysis in the contemporary press or ratification debates.[16] The most substantive public comment came from James Madison, who spent four brief sentences in *The Federalist* No. 43 defending the proposed copyright power (and who misrepresented copyright's status in the common law in the process).[17]

Our best evidence about what the founding generation thought about the constitutional limits to copyright thus comes from what they *did* almost immediately following ratification: they passed the 1790 Copyright Act. To judge from that statute, they did not think copyright deserved very long or broad protections. As mentioned earlier in this chapter the 1790 act offered a copyright term of only 14 years with the option to renew for another 14.[18] By way of comparison, the basic term in the present act runs for the author's life plus 70 years.[19] The 1790 act afforded copyright holders but few remedies—only statutory damages and the destruction of infringing works.[20] Remedies in the current act include destruction of infringing copies and devices used in infringement,[21] statutory damages or actual damages and unjust profits,[22] costs and attorneys' fees,[23] bars on the importation of infringing articles,[24] the power to subpoena digital service providers to disclose the identity of alleged infringers,[25] and criminal sanctions including fines and imprisonment.[26]

Most surprisingly, the 1790 act covered only maps, charts, and books.[27] The present act, in contrast, covers all kinds of graphic and literary works, as well as songs, plays, dances, sculptures, movies, sound recordings, architectural works, computer programs, and indeed any original fixed expression of authorship, no matter what its form.[28] Under current law, even a grocery list can win a copyright. Although some modern modes of expression might have surprised the Founders, they certainly knew about the charms of songs, plays, dances, sculptures, and architectural works. Why did they not include those works in the scope of the 1790 act?

The Founders seem to have taken very seriously the constitutional mandate that copyright promote "Science and the useful Arts"—words that, then as now, most plainly refer not to mere pretty fripperies but rather to useful, even technical works. The 1790 act's concern for maps and charts plainly reflects that tough-minded and characteristically American philosophy. So does the act's concern for books, which the Founders probably considered to be utilitarian tools more than amusing diversions. Novels had not yet risen to prominence in that early literary era, after all; the first American novel, William Hill Brown's *The Power of Sympathy*, appeared only a year before passage of the 1790 act (and even its ad copy promised the practical goal of exposing "the fatal consequences of seduction").[29] Judging from the titles in libraries and on sale, fiction made up only a small portion of the books available in late 18th-century America.[30] The Founders evidently aimed to have copyright serve the practical needs of a growing nation rather than the creative urges of songwriters, painters, sculptors, and other artists.

Whether the narrow scope of the 1790 act came from timidity, considerations of public policy, or respect for constitutional limits we cannot say for certain. The historical context and legislative history of the 1790 act shows no consideration that music, pictures, dances, plays, sculptures, or the like might qualify as "Writings" by "Authors" liable to "promote the Progress of Science and useful Arts," as the Constitution specifies.[31] Regardless, it was not for ignorance or want of love that the Founders denied copyrights to the pure arts.

The Founders' unwillingness to give the government any but absolutely necessary and proper powers reveals profound wisdom. If we want to reform copyright's excesses, we could hardly do better than abolishing the present statute, together with Title I of the

DMCA and various other para-copyright laws of dubious constitutionality, and reinstating the 1790 act in its place. We still honor the text of the Founders' Constitution, after all; why not extend a similar honor to the Founders' copyright? This we should do not out of simple admiration for those great men. Though paeans to them often veer into hagiography,[32] the Founders indisputably knew a great deal about the fundamental principles of governance. Their version of copyright offers the virtues of restraint, practicality, and fidelity to the Constitution.

Although technological advances have introduced new forms of expression since the 1790 act's passage, they have not rendered its parsimonious approach to copyright any less relevant. As noted above, the Founders did not extend copyright to music, painting, sculpture, and other arts well known and widely appreciated in 1790. Had photographs, movies, and sound recordings existed at the time, they would doubtless have met the same stony refusal.[33]

Nor can we impugn the wisdom of the 1790 Copyright Act by citing the wealth of expressive works that have poured forth under later, decidedly more expansive statutes. To the contrary, that the Founders declined to coddle merely aesthetic works even in an age of comparative cultural poverty shows all the more how seriously they took the Constitution's admonition that copyright serve "Science and useful Arts" (an admonition that the Supreme Court now effectively refuses to enforce).[34] Furthermore, that we now enjoy unprecedented access to songs, pictures, movies, and other such entertaining diversions should make it all the easier for us to reclaim the Founders' decidedly flinty approach to copyright. Perhaps we can credit copyright's latter-day growth for generating a flood of original expressions; perhaps not. Regardless, we no longer face a drought of artistic works. We can now refocus copyright on practical concerns and still have our fun.

Reviving the 1790 act would have a bold effect on US copyright law, admittedly, and ruffle more than a few feathers. That merely demonstrates how far the present regime has strayed from its constitutional roots, however. As the Founders well understood, responsible lawmakers must cabin federal power within strict boundaries, ensure that it serves the general welfare, and safeguard it against capture by a privileged few. On all those counts, successors to the 1790 act have failed. To save copyright's future, we must return to its past.

WITHDRAW THE US FROM THE BERNE CONVENTION

To revive the 1790 Copyright Act would put the United States in violation of the Berne Convention for the Protection of Literary and Artistic Works, an international agreement that imposes certain minimum standards for copyright and requires each signatory country to extend to foreign copyright holders the same privileges it gives its own nationals. The 1790 act requires that copyright holders fulfill certain formalities to win and retain its privileges—requirements inconsistent with the Berne Convention.[35] The 1790 act also offends the Berne Convention by allowing only citizens and residents of the United States to win domestically enforceable copyrights.[36]

More fundamentally, the Founders' characteristically American approach to copyright—requiring that it serve practical ends and sharply limiting its power—contrasts with the Continental philosophy underlying the Berne Convention, which instead aims to protect original expressive works as if they were extensions of their creators' personalities. After the US joined the convention in 1988, federal lawmakers amended the copyright statute to conform to the new international standards.[37] Reviving the 1790 act would change all that. The Berne Convention would have to adapt to the US reforms or, more likely, the US would have to withdraw from the Berne Convention.

That reviving the 1790 Copyright Act would break the Berne Convention's grip on US law represents a feature, not a bug. The US resisted joining the Berne Convention for more than 100 years before the copyright lobby, attracted by the prospect of winning greater access to foreign markets, and the legal intelligentsia, enchanted by European theorizing, prevailed. US copyright policy should not heed foreign copyright markets, however; it should aim only to ensure that US copyright holders find domestic markets profitable enough to stimulate the supply of original expressive works. Washington should focus on how well Hollywood does at home, in other words. Because US laws cannot have extraterritorial reach, foreign infringements cannot cause any losses cognizable under the Copyright Act. Guaranteeing domestic copyright holders additional profits from markets abroad simply adds another layer of icing to an already overloaded cake. If public policy concerns meant more than public choice pressures, in fact, US lawmakers would have balanced the Berne Convention's market-opening effects by trimming copyright's privileges (they did nothing of the sort, of course).

ESCAPE FROM COPYRIGHT TO THE COMMON LAW VIA THE MISUSE DOCTRINE

The prior two reforms, reviving the 1790 Copyright Act and leaving the Berne Convention, charge copyright headfirst. Copyright reform via the misuse doctrine, in contrast, employs a subtle bit of legal jiujitsu. The key to this strategy comes from recognizing something only implicit in the case law: courts applying the misuse doctrine tend to bar only offending copyright claims, leaving contract and other common-law rights unaffected. That insight opens an escape route from our present world, where copyright's statutory privileges comprehensively regulate expressive works, to a world where common-law rules alone control.

What is copyright's misuse doctrine? It operates as a defense for copyright infringement, applicable when a "copyright is being used in a manner violative of the public policy embodied in the grant of a copyright."[38] As that formulation suggests, the exact parameters of the copyright misuse doctrine remain a bit uncertain. The US Supreme Court has only hinted at the doctrine[39] and federal lawmakers have not codified it.[40] It arose as and remains a doctrine recognized only in many various lower court opinions.[41] *Alcatel USA, Inc. v. DGI Techs., Inc.*, for instance, found misuse in a copyright holder's practice of licensing its software for use only on its own hardware.[42] Similarly, the court in *Practice Mgmt. Info. Corp. v. Am. Med. Ass'n* held that a license preventing the use of alternative works gave the copyright holder an unfair advantage over its competitors, giving rise to misuse.[43] Judging from those and other cases, copyright misuse occurs when a copyright holder wields a licensing agreement to stifle otherwise permissible competition,[44] inhibits what the fair use defense plainly allows,[45] or otherwise combines copyright's privileges with common-law rights in an unseemly manner.[46]

How can misuse doctrine open an escape from copyright? The doctrine bars claims of copyright infringement that arise under conditions of misuse.[47] It does not, however, bar claims premised on violations of common-law rights, such as trade secrets or the contractual terms of a license.[48] In effect, misuse doctrine corrects the overweening power that results from combining copyright privileges with common-law rights, by negating only the former. Suppose for instance that a copyright holder wrongly tried to squelch rights protected by the First Amendment and the fair use doctrine by including in its license a clause forbidding public criticism of the work. A court might remedy that misuse by denying the considerable enforcement powers afforded by the Copyright Act even while leaving the underlying contract in force. In practical terms, the dispute would become a matter of state contract law rather than federal legislation. Repeated applications of the same doctrine in other cases would eventually encourage the development of business models premised solely on contract law, tort law, trade secret law, and other common-law devices. Misuse thus opens an escape from a world where copyright comprehensively regulates access to expressive works to one where only common-law rules apply.

Courts invoking copyright misuse have not evidently intended to open an exit to the common law, granted; it takes a discerning eye to even spot the phenomenon. It nonetheless presents an inviting prospect for copyright reform. Suppose for instance that the misuse defense prevents a copyright holder from enforcing his statutory privileges. Depending on his business model, he may find it more worthwhile to continue forgoing his copyright claims and instead rely on his common-law contract, tort, or property rights. If that experiment proves successful, others might emulate it. Copyright's misuse doctrine could thereby gently encourage would-be copyright holders to learn how to live—perhaps even to thrive—without the privileges offered by federal lawmakers. The Copyright Act would become less and less relevant as creators find more flexible and efficient ways to market their expressive works. Best of all, copyright reform could proceed through the courts, on a case-by-case basis, without any need to sway federal lawmakers.

FOCUS COPYRIGHT POLICY ON CONSUMERS' COSTS, NOT PRODUCERS' PROFITS

Copyright reform should include not just changes to statutes, treaties, and legal theories, but also changes to the way that we approach copyright policy. Here, we should put consumers before producers. In other words, copyright policy should focus on whether consumers have ready access to original expressive works, and not on whether producers earn sufficient profits. Copyright policy has done its job if average Americans can access a cornucopia of stories, music, videos, and other expressive works (for instance, by typing a few keys on an Internet-enabled device). Lobbyists thus entirely miss the point when they cite the copyright industry's size and power as proof that lawmakers should make copyright stronger still.[49] They should instead argue—if they honestly can—that consumers do not enjoy adequate access to creative works.

This is not to say that the profits of creators and publishers mean nothing to copyright policy, of course. We count on their greed to have a stimulating effect, driving them to produce more expressive works than they otherwise would. Ultimately, though, copyright's private incentives serve merely as a means to a public end. Copyright policy should focus not on special interests but on promoting "Science and useful Arts" and ultimately "the general Welfare," its sole constitutional goals.[50] Perhaps those who lobby for more and greater copyright powers honestly believe that their efforts will redound to the greater good; perhaps they care only about how much benefit they can deliver to their clients. We need not settle that question. We need only make sure that consumers—not producers—remain the ultimate focus of copyright policy.

Before lawmakers decide how powerful to make copyright's privileges, therefore, they should first decide whether the public wants for new books, songs, movies, computer programs, and so forth. Absent compelling proof of a market failure in the supply of original expressive works, there can be no justification for increasing the length or breadth of copyright. It is not simply a program for making the copyright industry rich. Whether consumers have genuinely suffered from having too few options in the market for copyrightable works must in all fairness remain a question of fact. It is a case the copyright lobby will find difficult to make, however.

RECONCEIVE COPYRIGHT AS INTELLECTUAL *PRIVILEGE*

To reform the way that copyright works, we have to change the way that people think about it. And to change the way that people think about copyright, we have to change the way they talk about it. To improve copyright, therefore, we should reconceive it not as a form of intellectual *property* but as a form of intellectual *privilege*. The latter term better describes copyright's legal basis and protects traditional property rights from suffering rhetorical erosion. Plus, we can keep calling copyright IP.

Why would anyone refer to copyrights as *property* in the first place? Bad philosophy deserves some of the blame. Locke's "Second Treatise of Government" famously justified property rights in these three steps: you own yourself; you thus own your labor; you thus own the things with which you mix your labor.[51] So far, so good, but some of Locke's followers have applied his natural rights theory to defend copyright.[52] For that gambit to work, we would have to accept the noumenal realm of ideas as a "thing" that creators can mix with their labor—writers homestead territory in the land of the muses, one might say. Locke, at least, was not willing to go that far.

In neither the "Second Treatise" nor elsewhere did Locke give copyright shelter under his theory of property. His illustrations cite real things from the real world—acorns, fields, and the like. Locke evidently viewed copyright as no more than a device for promoting the public good, and a dangerous one at that.[53] He described the copyright of his own day—the Stationer's Company—as a "manifest ... invasion of the trade, liberty, and property of the subject."[54] It thus proves perfectly apt that Locke did not claim any copyright in the "Second Treatise."[55]

In neither philosophy nor law do copyrights deserve to be called *property*. We enjoy rights to our persons and *tangible* properties even in a state of nature. Because we enjoy them only imperfectly, however, suffering the injustices occasioned by a want of a common legal authority, we voluntarily cede some portion of those natural rights when we institute civil government. On that, a social contract account, property rights arise naturally; states come after the fact and only in the service of protecting our extant rights. But copyright cannot exist in a state of nature; it relies on state legislation. We did not bring copyright to the table when we entered into the social contract because we did not enjoy any such intangible right. Nor can we take it with us if we walk away. Copyright thus does not qualify as natural the way other property rights do. Nor is copyright a property right recognized by the common law.[56]

Copyright has property-like features, granted; copyrighted works can be registered, bought and sold, licensed, donated, mortgaged, or abandoned.[57] These represent praiseworthy features, as they improve the efficiency of copyright policy in much the same way that tradable pollution permits, food stamps, and school vouchers have improved the policies they touch. All this does not suffice to make *property* an apt name for copyright, however, especially given that copyright lacks many of the features that characterize traditional forms of property.

Copyright, as purely a creature of statute, can change form at lawmakers' whims. Unlike other forms of property, it must expire after a specified time.[58] On one hand, the Copyright Act empowers authors to terminate rights that they have freely and willingly granted to others without paying compensation to the losing grantees—a notion alien to the law of property (and thankfully so).[59] On the other hand, though the exact question remains as yet unlitigated, *Zoltek Corp. v. United States* strongly suggests that copyright does not qualify for just compensation under the Fifth Amendment's takings clause.[60] Whereas property owners enjoy very strong protections against trespass, copyright holders must suffer many and various uses that the act excuses as "fair."[61]

Property is neither an accurate label for copyright nor one we have to embrace by default. We can more accurately label copyright a *privilege*—a statutory exception to common-law rights and obligations that vests its holder with special powers and immunities.[62]

In addition to wayward philosophy and legal mislabeling, we can blame the copyright lobby for invoking the language of property opportunistically. "We just want to protect private property from being pillaged," claimed Jack Valenti, president of the Motion Picture Association of America, when he pled (unsuccessfully) for lawmakers to redesign televisions to prevent consumers from recording programs.[63] Hilary Rosen, president of the Recording Industry Association of America, lobbied against the unauthorized distribution of sound recordings, saying, "No one wants their property taken from them and distributed without their permission."[64] Lars Ulrich, drummer for Metallica, testified before Congress that the advent of digital music downloads "sounds to me like old-fashioned trafficking in stolen goods."[65] Equating copyrights with property and infringements with theft may make for effective rhetoric, but it does not make much philosophical or legal sense.

The policy issues bound up with copyright are too complicated to resolve by simply invoking the label *property*. Copyright is not like the property rights protected by the common law for this fundamental reason: Expressive works are non-rivalrous in consumption. This is not a matter of law, but of physics. You may leave an artist hungry if you eat her bread, but you cannot silence her by singing her song. It does not obliterate that distinction to observe that at some scales, under special conditions, even tangible property can accommodate marginally greater uses at no greater marginal cost, as when someone sneaks into a near-empty theater to watch a movie. Copyright's non-rivalrousness runs front to back and end to end, at all scales and under all conditions.

Friends of property rights, especially, should resist letting the copyright lobby run off with their word. Think of *property* as akin to a service mark, one that designates not a repair shop or beauty salon but a pillar of our legal culture. Where would we find ourselves if overuse of *property* were to bleed the word of all meaning? Nowhere good. We can protect the integrity of property, as both a word and a legal concept, by speaking of copyright with the language of privilege.

Instead of *intellectual property*, say *intellectual privilege*. Speak of copyright *holders* rather than *owners*, and talk about how the statute vests them not with *protections from* infringers but with *restrictions on* all the public. Adopting more accurate terminology can save us from unexamined misconceptions about copyright, and open our eyes to the possibilities of reform.

To say that copyright is not property is not to treat it with contempt. We owe great debts to great artists and should expect to pay generously if we want more of the same. We can pay due respect to copyright without calling it property, however, treating it much as we do speed limits, income taxes, and other statutes passed not to protect fundamental rights but to coordinate social life and promote the general welfare. We might follow such laws out of cool logic, ardent patriotism, unreflective habit, grudging acceptance, or even simple fear. Respect for property rights has little to do with that, though.

FREEDOM'S ECHO

Despite copyright's recent excesses, we owe it our thanks. It originated as a good-faith attempt to achieve noble goals and for many years quietly did its job. US copyright law deserves credit for encouraging an outpouring of original expressive works, bequeathing us with a rich cultural heritage. We thus have good reason to respect copyright. Recent trends, shocking anecdotes, and the inexorable logic of lobbying increasingly give us reason to fear copyright, though.

Who can claim that every word from their lips falls fresh, uncolored by any copying? Humans *must* copy each other; communication relies on echoed words, messages, and thoughts. We even express ourselves through our mutual unoriginality when, joining our voices in protest or celebration, we copy each other for a common cause. Copyright thus bestows authors and their assigns with potentially dangerous powers over the very foundations of human society.

Copyright's yoke seldom chafes, granted. Enforcement costs and the fair use defense keep the sharp end of the Copyright Act pointed away from most of us, most of the time. Make no mistake, though; copyright law does not count on sweet persuasion to discourage infringement. Samantha Tumpach could tell you that. Copyright's statutory privileges come only at hazard to our natural and common-law rights. To preserve our freedoms, therefore, we must reform copyright.

NOTES

1. Dan Rozek, "Woman Arrested for Trying to Record 'Twilight' on Digital Camera," *Chicago Sun-Times*, December 2, 2009, http://web.archive.org/web/20091205034644/http://www.suntimes.com/news/metro/1916606,twilight-taping-arrest-movie-120209.article.
2. Ibid.
3. Aliyah Shahid, "*Twilight* Taper, Samantha Tumpach, Sues Illinois Theater after Taping *Twilight Saga: New Moon*," *New York Daily*

News, June 29, 2010, http://articles.nydailynews.com/2010-06-29 /news/27068531_1_new-moon-twilight-saga-illinois-woman.

4. See, for example, Pamela Samuelson, "Reforming Copyright Is Possible," *Chronicle of Higher Education*, July 9, 2012, http://chronicle .com/article/Reforming-Copyright-Is/132751/ (advocating measures designed to make collective licensing of books easier); Lawrence Lessig, "In Defense of Piracy," *Wall Street Journal*, October 11, 2008, http://online.wsj.com/article/SB122367645363324303.html (offering five reforms that would deregulate but not fundamentally change copyright).

5. See, for example, Cary Sherman, "Copyright Bills Won't Kill the Internet," *CNET*, November 8, 2011, http://news.cnet.com/8301 -1023_3-57320417-93/riaa-chief-copyright-bills-wont-kill-the -internet/?tag=cnetRiver (defending proposed legislation targeting "rogue" infringing websites).

6. See, for example, Stephan Kinsella, "The SOPA Wake-Up Call to Abolish Copyright," *InformationLiberation* (blog), February 1, 2012, http:// www.informationliberation.com/?id=38216 (describing the anti-copyright views of some activists).

7. In truth, of course, the US did abolish slavery in steps. The Emancipation Proclamation of 1862 affected only rebel states, leaving slavery legal in the District of Columbia, Missouri, Kentucky, Maryland, and other parts of the Union. Only with passage of the Thirteenth Amendment, three years later, did slaves in the North win freedom.

8. U.S. Constitution, art. 1, sec. 8, cl.#8. Although some authorities cite only "the Progress of Science" as copyright's constitutional aim, reserving "useful Arts" as a concern for patent law, the better reading holds off on giving the clause a two-track interpretation until after "for limited Times to," a single provision that applies to "Authors . . . Writings" and "Inventors . . . Discoveries" alike. Malla Pollack, "Unconstitutional Incontestability? The Intersection of the Intellectual Property and Commerce Clauses of the Constitution: Beyond a Critique of *Shakespeare Co. v. Silstar Corp.*," *Seattle University Law Review* 18 (1995): 259, 282–83.

9. *Copyright Act of 1790*, 1 Stat. 124 (1790), reprinted in *Copyright Office,*

Library of Congress, Bulletin No. 3 (Revised), Copyright Enactments: Laws Passed in the United States Since 1783 Relating to Copyright, at 22, 22 (1973).

10. US Copyright Office, Circular 92: Copyright Law of the United States and Related Laws Contained in Title 17 of the United States Code, December 2011, http://www.copyright.gov/title17/circ92.pdf.

11. 17 C.F.R. 37 §§ 201.1-270-.5 (2012), http://www.copyright.gov/title37/.

12. Terms come from Copyright Act of 1790, 1 Stat. 124 § 1 (1790); An Act to Amend the Several Acts Respecting Copyrights, 4 Stat. 436 §§ 1–2 (February 3, 1831); Copyright Act of 1909, 17 U.S.C. § 23 (1909); 17 U.S.C. § 302(a) (1994) (see also 17 U.S.C. § 302[c]: works authored anonymously, pseudonymously, or for hire get the lesser of publication plus 75 years or creation plus 100 years); Sonny Bono Copyright Term Extension Act, Public Law 105–298, 112 Stat. 2827 (1998), codified at 17 U.S.C. §§ 302(a)–(b) (see also 17 U.S.C. § 302[c]: works made anonymously, pseudonymously, or for hire get the lesser of publication plus 95 years or creation plus 120 years). The figure conservatively assumes that authors create their works at age 35 and live for 70 years. The figure's overhanging ledges reflect retroactive extensions of copyright terms.

13. Timothy B. Lee, "Copyright Enforcement and the Internet: We Just Haven't Tried Hard Enough?," Ars Technica (blog), February 14, 2012, http://arstechnica.com/tech-policy/2012/02/copyright-enforcement -and-the-internet-we-just-havent-tried-hard-enough/.

14. Owings v. Speed, 18 U.S. 192, 194 (1820) (holding that the Constitution did not replace the Articles of Confederation until March 4, 1789); Copyright Act of 1790, 1 Stat. 124 (1790).

15. U.S. Constitution, art 1, sec. 8, cl.#8. See also note 8.

16. Edward C. Walterscheid, "To Promote the Progress of Science and Useful Arts: The Background and Origin of the Intellectual Property Clause of the United States Constitution," Journal of Intellectual Property Law 2 (1994): 23–56 (describing the paucity of evidence from the Convention and state ratifying conventions); Karl Fenning, "The Origin of the Patent and Copyright Clause of the Constitution," Georgetown Law Journal 17 (1929): 109, 114 (reviewing the evidence and concluding that the clause "apparently aroused substantially no

controversy either in the Convention or among the States adopting the Constitution").

17. Tom W. Bell, "Escape from Copyright: Market Success vs. Statutory Failure in the Protection of Expressive Works," *University of Cincinnati Law Review* 69 (2001): 741, 771 (explaining that, intentionally or not, Madison relied on bad precedent).

18. 1 Stat. 124 (1790), § 1.

19. 17 U.S.C. § 302.

20. 1 Stat. 124 (1790), § 2.

21. 17 U.S.C. §§ 503, 506(b).

22. 17 U.S.C. § 504.

23. 17 U.S.C. § 505.

24. 17 U.S.C. § 602.

25. 17 U.S.C. § 512(h).

26. 17 U.S.C. § 506.

27. 1 Stat. 124 § 1.

28. 17 U.S.C. § 102.

29. Patricia Crain, "Print and Everyday Life in the Eighteenth Century," in *Perspectives on American Book History: Artifacts and Commentary*, ed. Scott E. Casper, Joanne D. Chaison, and Jeffrey D. Groves (Cambridge, MA: Univ. of Massachusetts Press, 2002), 47, 74.

30. See Hugh Amory, "Appendix One: A Note on Statistics," in *A History of the Book in America*, ed. Hugh Amory and David D. Hall, vol. 1, *The Colonial Book in the Atlantic World* (Cambridge, UK: Cambridge Univ. Press, 2000), 511. Amory reports that in America from 1640–1790, imprints of practical and instructional genres, such as government works (7182), sermons (3192), almanacs (1977), schoolbooks (1085), and academic dissertations (323), greatly outnumbered imprints of poetry (1854), hymnals (254), psalm books (253), satires (201), plays (111), and novels (38). See also Julie Hedgepeth Williams, *The Significance of the Printed Word in Early America* (Westport, CT: Greenwood Publishing, 1999), 17–20. Williams describes the typical contents of libraries and private collections in 18th-century America.

31. Oren Bracha, "Commentary on the Copyright Act 1790," in *Primary Sources on Copyright (1450–1900)*, ed. L. Bently and M. Kretschmer,

2008, http://www.copyrighthistory.org.

32. See, for example, Creased Comics, "'Washington,'" YouTube video, 2:24, posted by "boomtasticracing," February 13, 2009, http://www.youtube.com/watch?v=Iqhsot3mk7Q. The video claims George Washington was "six-foot-eight and weighed a f*cking ton."

33. Perhaps the Founders would have afforded computer programs greater solicitude, as worthy promoters of science and useful arts. If so, they could have kept the 1790 act's reference to "books" and followed the present practice of classifying computer programs as literary works.

34. See Eldred v. Ashcroft, 537 U.S. 186, 211-12 (2003) (deferring to legislative judgments about whether copyright serves constitutional ends).

35. Berne Convention, art. 5(2).

36. 1 Stat. 124 § 1.

37. See Berne Convention Implementation Act of 1988, Public Law 100–568, 102 Stat. 2853 (Oct. 31, 1988), effective March 1, 1989.

38. Lasercomb Am., Inc. v. Reynolds, 911 F.2d 970, 978 (4th Cir. 1990).

39. See United States v. Loew's, Inc., 371 U.S. 38, 50 (1962) (stating that "the principles underlying our Paramount Pictures decision have general application to tying arrangements involving copyrighted products"); United States v. Paramount Pictures, Inc., 334 U.S. 131, 158 (1948) (approving an injunction against certain copyright licensing practices on the grounds that the practices "add to the monopoly of the copyright in violation of the principle of the patent cases involving tying clauses").

40. But see Tom W. Bell, "Codifying Copyright's Misuse Doctrine," Utah Law Review, 2007, 573 (proposing an amendment to the Copyright Act clarifying the misuse defense).

41. See, e.g., DSC Commc'ns Corp. v. Pulse Commc'ns, Inc., 170 F.3d 1354, 1368 (Fed. Cir. 1999) (recognizing "copyright misuse is a defense to a claim of copyright infringement"); Alcatel USA, Inc. v. DGI Techs., Inc., 166 F.3d 772, 792 (5th Cir. 1999) (holding the same); Practice Mgmt. Info. Corp. v. Am. Med. Ass'n, 121 F.3d 516, 520 (9th Cir. 1997) (holding the same); Lasercomb Am., Inc. v. Reynolds, 911 F.2d 970, 976 (4th Cir. 1990) (holding the same). See also Rosemont Enters., Inc. v. Random

House, Inc., 366 F.2d 303, 311 (2d Cir. 1966) (Chief Justice Lumbard, concurring) (recognizing that the doctrine of unclean hands should bar enforcement of a copyright used to "restrict the dissemination of information about persons in the public eye even though those concerned may not welcome the resulting publicity").

42. 166 F.3d 772, 793–94 (5th Cir. 1999).

43. 121 F.3d 516, 520–21 (9th Cir. 1997).

44. See Alcatel, 166 F.3d at 793–94 (5th Cir. 1999); *Practice Mgmt.*, 121 F.3d at 520–21; *Lasercomb*, 911 F.2d at 977–79.

45. Bond v. Blum, 317 F.3d 385, 397–98 (7th Cir. 2003) (affirming the trial court's finding of misuse where the plaintiff brought an infringement suit "to suppress the underlying facts of his copyrighted work rather than to safeguard its creative expression"); Video Pipeline, Inc. v. Buena Vista Home Entm't, Inc., 342 F.3d 191 (3d. Cir. 2003) (recognizing that a copyright owner might commit misuse in trying to enforce a license that prohibits criticism of copyright-restricted works, though affirming that the licenses in question had not gone that far).

46. Assessment Techs. of WI, LLC v. WIREdata, Inc., 350 F.3d 640, 647 (7th Cir. 2003) (explaining that it constitutes misuse "to use an infringement suit to obtain property protection, here in data, that copyright law clearly does not confer"). See also A&M Records, Inc. v. Napster, Inc., 239 F.3d 1004, 1026 (9th Cir. 2001) ("the misuse defense prevents copyright holders from leveraging their limited monopoly to allow them control of areas outside the monopoly"); *Lasercomb*, 911 F.2d at 979 ("the misuse arises from Lasercomb's attempt to use its copyright . . . to control competition in an area outside the copyright").

47. See, e.g., *Lasercomb*, 911 F.2d at 979 n.22 ("Lasercomb is free to bring a suit for infringement once it has purged itself of the misuse").

48. Bell, "Escape from Copyright," 800.

49. See, e.g., Steven E. Siwek, *Copyright Industries in the U.S. Economy: The 2003-2007 Report* (International Intellectual Property Alliance, June 2009), http://www.iipa.com/pdf/IIPASiwekReport2003-07.pdf, 4–5 (reporting that US copyright industries had growth rates well above the US economy as a whole during the studied period).

50. U.S. Constitution, art. 1, sec. 8, cl.#8, preamble.

51. John Locke, "The Second Treatise of Government" (1690), in *Two Treatises of Government* by John Locke, ed. Peter Laslett (Cambridge, UK: Cambridge Univ. Press, 1963).

52. See, e.g., Ayn Rand, "Patents and Copyrights," in *Capitalism: The Unknown Ideal*, by Ayn Rand et al. (New York: Signet, 1967), 130; Herbert Spencer, *The Principles of Ethics*, ed. T. Machan (Indianapolis: Liberty Fund, 1978) (originally published 1893), 2:121; Lysander Spooner, "A Letter to Scientists and Inventors, on the Science of Justice, and Their Right of Perpetual Property in Their Discoveries and Inventions," in *The Collected Works of Lysander Spooner*, ed. C. Shively (Weston, MA: M and S Press, 1971), 3:68.

53. See Ronan Deazley, *Rethinking Copyright* (Cheltonham, UK: Edward Elgar Publishing, Inc., 2006), 143–44n32 (reading Locke's correspondence to indicate that "Locke himself did not consider that his theory of property extended to intellectual properties such as copyrights and patents").

54. John Locke, "Observations on the Printing Act under Consideration in Parliament in 1694," in *The Life of John Locke, with Extracts from His Correspondence, Journals, and Common-Place Books*, by Peter King (1830), 1:373, 386.

55. Locke could not have done so even had he wanted to, given the contemporary requirement that authors identify themselves and his lifelong refusal to take credit for the "Second Treatise."

56. The so-called *common-law copyright* is neither common (as it appears in very few decisions) nor law (given that the act now expressly preempts it) nor copyright (because it concerns only first publication). Howard B. Abrams, "The Historic Foundation of American Copyright Law: Exploding the Myth of Common Law Copyright," *Wayne Law Review* 29 (1983): 1119, 1128–33.

57. See 17 U.S.C. §§ 201–5.

58. 17 U.S.C. § 302–5.

59. 17 U.S.C. §§ 203, 304(c), and 304(d). If more straightforward takings of copyrights do not qualify for just compensation under the Fifth Amendment, it seems very unlikely that regulatory takings, which scarcely get any recognition with regard to tangible property, would.

60. 442 F.3d 1345 (Fed. Cir. 2006), *reh'g den*. 464 F.3d 1335, 1350 (Fed. Cir. 2006) (holding that patent infringement by the federal government does not constitute a taking under the Fifth Amendment), cert. den. 127 S. Ct. 2936, 168 L. Ed. 2d 262 (2007).

61. 17 U.S.C. § 107.

62. Tom W. Bell, "Copyright as Intellectual ~~Property~~ Privilege," *Syracuse Law Review* 58 (2007): 523.

63. Edmund Sanders and Jube Shiver Jr., "Digital TV Copyright Concerns Tentatively Resolved by Group," *Los Angeles Times*, April 26, 2002 (quoting Valenti's speech before a congressional committee).

64. Doug Bedell, "Piracy Enforcement Flounders with Rise of MP3," *Dallas Morning News*, Aug. 11, 1999 (quoting Rosen).

65. *The Future of Digital Music: Is There an Upside to Downloading? Hearings on Copyright Issues and Digital Music on the Internet Before the Senate Judiciary Comm.*, 106th Cong. (2000) (statement of Lars Ulrich, drummer for Metallica).

Acknowledgments

HIS COLLECTION OF essays is something I have wanted to produce since Adam Thierer and Wayne Crews published *Copy Fights* ten years ago. Helping to put that volume together, I saw firsthand how divisive the issue of copyright can be among libertarians and conservatives. The way I saw it, though, there was much on which we could all agree if we took a practical view of copyright grounded in public choice. This book is an attempt to begin to forge a new pragmatic consensus.

I, therefore, have to first thank Adam Thierer for his mentorship and inspiration over all these years. He does not share my optimism that a consensus can be reached, but that has made him an invaluable sounding board who has helped sharpen my thinking on the issue. For that, I'm very grateful.

My sincerest thanks also go to the contributors: Reihan Salam, Patrick Ruffini, David Post, Tim Lee, Christina Mulligan, Eli Dourado, and Tom Bell. If there ever was a dream team of "cyber libertarian" thinkers on copyright, this is it. I am very lucky to have been able to assemble them here. Special thanks go to Eli Dourado, who, as an office neighbor and frequent lunch partner, has greatly influenced my thinking on copyright and other issues.

This book would have not been possible without the hard work of some of the amazing folks at the Mercatus Center at George Mason University with whom I have the privilege of working. Chief among these is James Broughel, whose eternal patience while managing the logistics of this project are sincerely appreciated by me and all the contributors. Garrett Brown and Emma Elliott have made book projects like this one not just a reality, but a pleasure, and for that I am grateful. Thanks also go to Ted Bolema, whose common sense editing was invaluable. And finally thanks to Kate Martin and Taylor Barkley without whose hard work Adam, Eli, and I would merely be talking to ourselves.

I'd like to thank Jim Harper for his encouragement and support as well as comments on an early draft, Ryan Radia for always thoughtful critiques, Dan Rothschild for helpful comments, and my wonderful wife, Kathleen O'Hearn, for her unending love and cheer, which make everything worthwhile.

Arlington, Virginia, October 2012

About the Editor

JERRY BRITO is a senior research fellow at the Mercatus Center at George Mason University and the director of its Technology Policy Program. He also serves as adjunct professor of law at Mason. His research focuses on technology and telecommunications policy, government transparency and accountability, and the regulatory process. He has written for both online and print publications, including the *Wall Street Journal,* the *New York Times, Reason,* Wired .com, Ars Technica, and the *Atlantic.* He lives in Arlington, Virginia, with his wife, Kathleen O'Hearn.

About the Contributors

TOM W. BELL is a professor at Chapman University School of Law and an adjunct fellow of the Cato Institute. His writings include *Intellectual Privilege: Copyright, Common Law, and the Common Good* (Mercatus Center at George Mason University, forthcoming); *Regulators' Revenge: The Future of Telecommunications Deregulation* (Cato Institute), which he edited with Solveig Singleton; and many papers and articles. After earning a JD from the University of Chicago, Bell practiced law in Silicon Valley and Washington, DC. He began teaching in 1995, took a year's leave of absence to serve as the Cato Institute's director of telecommunications and technology studies, and joined Chapman University School of Law in 1998. Bell and his family live in San Clemente, California.

ELI DOURADO is a research fellow at the Mercatus Center at George Mason University with the Technology Policy Program, and a PhD candidate in the Department of Economics at Mason. His research focuses on the economics and political economy of technology. Before joining Mercatus, Dourado worked at the Bureau of Economic Analysis and the US House of Representatives. He lives in Arlington, Virginia, with his wife and dog.

TIMOTHY B. LEE is an adjunct scholar at the Cato Institute. He covers technology policy for Ars Technica, with a particular focus on patent and copyright law, privacy, free speech, and open government. While at Princeton earning his master's degree in computer science, Lee was a coauthor of RECAP, a Firefox plugin that helps users liberate public documents from the federal judiciary's paywall. He has written for both online and print publications, including Slate.com, *Reason,* Wired.com, and the *New York Times.* He and his wife live in Philadelphia.

CHRISTINA MULLIGAN is a postdoctoral associate in law and a lecturer in law at the Information Society Project at Yale Law School. She has written for the *Washington Post,* Ars Technica, and Balkinization, and has journal articles forthcoming in the *Tennessee Law Review,* the *SMU Law Review,* and the *New York University Annual Survey of American Law.* She holds BA and JD degrees from Harvard University. She lives in New Haven, Connecticut.

DAVID G. POST is professor of law at the Beasley School of Law at Temple University, where he teaches intellectual property law and the law of cyberspace. He is also a fellow at the Center for Democracy and Technology and the Institute for Information Law and Policy at New York Law School, an adjunct scholar at the Cato Institute, and a regular contributor to the influential *Volokh Conspiracy* blog. He is the author of *In Search of Jefferson's Moose: Notes on the State of Cyberspace* (Oxford), which won the 2010 Green Bag "Exemplary Legal Writing" prize, and a coauthor of *Cyberlaw: Problems of Policy and Jurisprudence in the Information Age* (West), with Paul Schiff Berman, Patricia Bellia, and Brett Frischmann. He has served as a law clerk to Justice Ruth Bader Ginsburg on both the DC Circuit Court of Appeals and the US Supreme Court. He and his wife, Nancy, split their time between Washington, DC, and Marlboro, VT.

PATRICK RUFFINI is president of Engage, a digital media firm with clients including Fortune 500 companies, presidential and statewide candidates, technology startups, and issue advocacy campaigns. In the 2004 election, Ruffini served as webmaster for the Bush-Cheney campaign, managing day-to-day operations on the campaign's website. Ruffini is a graduate of the University of Pennsylvania, where he most enjoyed studying the history of presidential communication. He lives in Northern Virginia.

REIHAN SALAM is a policy advisor at Economics 21, a contributing editor at *National Review,* a Reuters opinion columnist, and a CNN contributor. He is the coauthor, with Ross Douthat, of *Grand New Party: How Republicans Can Win the Working Class and Save the American Dream* (Doubleday). Previously, he worked as an editorial researcher at *The New Republic* and the *New York Times,* a producer for NBC News, an associate editor at the *Atlantic,* and as a fellow at the New America Foundation. He lives in New York.

Index

Page numbers in *italics* indicate figures; the letter n following a page number indicates a note.

21432602R00081

Made in the USA
Lexington, KY
12 March 2013